WRITE TO $ELL:

HOW TO ADD DOLLARS TO YOUR INCOME WRITING NONFICTION ARTICLES AND GETTING THEM PUBLISHED

By

Ruth Wucherer

Published by
R&E PUBLISHERS
P. O. Box 2008
Saratoga, California 95070

Typesetting by
Stella Krebs

Library of Congress Cataloging-in-Publication Data

Wucherer, Ruth.
  Write to sell.

  1. Authorship--Vocational guidance. I. Title.
PN151.W83 1988   808'.02   87-90731
ISBN 0-88247-777-3

Copyright 1988
by
Ruth Wucherer

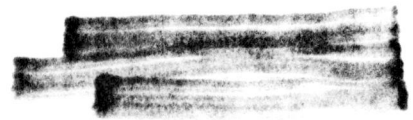

This book is dedicated

to nonfiction article writers

and would be writers

of nonfiction articles

OTHER BOOKS BY RUTH WUCHERER:

Travel Writing for Fun and Profit
     (also published and available from
            R&E Publishers)

How To Sell Your Crafts

TABLE OF CONTENTS

TABLE OF CONTENTS

INTRODUCTION 1

PART I   THINGS A NONFICTION WRITER SHOULD KNOW. . 3
- CHAPTER I   THE NONFICTION WRITER'S VOCABULARY .5
- CHAPTER II   RIGHTS AND THE WRITER 11
- CHAPTER III   WRITERS' CLUBS/ASSOCIATIONS 15

PART II   TECHNIQUES -- HOW TO DEVELOP, WRITE, TYPE AND MAIL YOUR ARTICLE -- PLUS PAYMENT FOR ARTICLES. 19
- CHAPTER IV   THE IMPORTANT QUERY LETTER 21
- CHAPTER V   INTERVIEWING TECHNIQUES 25
- CHAPTER VI   COMING UP WITH AN IDEA FOR AN ARTICLE 33
- CHAPTER VII   WRITING THE ARTICLE 37
- CHAPTER VIII   TYPING AND MAILING YOUR ARTICLE 51
- CHAPTER X   PAYMENT FOR ARTICLES, KEEPING TRACK OF SALES AND EXPENSES . .59

PART III   THE MARKETS -- OVER 250 PLACES (16 DIFFERENT CATEGORIES) TO SELL YOUR WORK PLUS SAMPLES OF MY PUBLISHED WORKS. 65
- CHAPTER XI   GENERAL INTEREST PUBLICATIONS. .67

CHAPTER XII	WOMEN'S PUBLICATIONS	77
CHAPTER XIII	TRAVEL AND INFLIGHT MARKETS	85
CHAPTER XIV	AUTO AND/OR TRAVEL CLUB PUBLICATIONS	97
CHAPTER XV	REGIONAL MARKETS	101
CHAPTER XVI	CAMPING AND RECREATIONAL VEHICLE PUBLICATIONS	115
CHAPTER XVII	SPORTS PUBLICATIONS	117
CHAPTER XVIII	MORE SPORTS PUBLICATIONS	125
CHAPTER XIX	HOBBY AND CRAFT PUBLICATIONS	139
CHAPTER XX	RELIGIOUS MARKETS	153
CHAPTER XXI	JUVENILE, TEEN AND YOUNG ADULT PUBLICATIONS	163
CHAPTER XXII	GARDEN AND HOME PUBLICATIONS	173
CHAPTER XXIII	NEWSPAPER AND NEWSPAPER MAGAZINES	179

ABOUT THE AUTHOR 185

INTRODUCTION

Write To $ell is a book for nonfiction article writers and those who are contemplating writing nonfiction articles. It is a how-to book, offering valuable instruction to both beginning and experienced nonfiction writers.

The author believes that one must not only be able to write the article but also be able to sell it. *Write To $ell* stresses techniques and gives the reader information on markets. The book is divided into three parts and has twenty-three chapters.

PART I covers Things A Nonfiction Writer Should Know. Chapter headings are The Nonfiction Writer's Vocabulary, Rights and the Writer, and Writers' Clubs/Associations.

PART II deals with techniques -- how to develop, write, type and mail your article plus payment for articles. It is the "nuts and bolts" section. Some of the chapter headings are: The Important Query Letter, Coming Up With An Idea for an Article, Typing and Mailing Your Article, and Photos Will Help To Sell Your Article.

PART III emphasizes The Markets -- over 150 places (12 different categories) to sell your work plus samples of the author's published works are included. Types of articles needed, length, payment rates, types and sizes of photos wanted, rights bought and addresses of each publication are given. The author wrote each editor to find out the most updated information. It is suggested that the reader write the publication again before preparing an article because some time has elapsed between the submission of this manuscript and the publication date of it.

Thanks to my typist, Sue Collins. She often gave me worthwhile suggestions on how to improve this manuscript.

Write To $ell will get you started in writing and selling your first nonfiction article and even your 1,000th article. There are hundreds of nonfiction article markets. The chances for a writer selling his or her work are excellent.

PART I

THINGS A NONFICTION WRITER SHOULD KNOW

CHAPTER I

THE NON FICTION WRITER'S VOCABULARY

Here is a vocabulary of 75 terms with which the nonfiction writer should be familiar. They are writing, printing and photographic terms listed alphabetically for your convenience.

Article - A written composition in prose, usually nonfiction, on a specific topic, forming an independent part of a book or other publication, as a newspaper and magazine.

Assignment - An editor asks a writer to do a specific article for which he or she usually names a payment for the completed manuscript.

B & W - Abbreviation for black and white photograph.

Bi-monthly - A publication that is published every two months.

Bi-weekly - A publication that comes out every two weeks.

Bold face - The dark form of a type family as compared to its medium and light forms. Usually chapter headings and sub-headings are set in this so they stand out.

Byline - The writer's name is put on the article, usually at the top but sometimes at the end of the article. Most writers usually receive a byline plus payment for their work.

Caption - A short description of a photograph.

Circulation - The number of people who subscribe to a publication.

Clips - If an editor is working with you for the first time, sometimes he or she requests clips of your previously published work.

Column inch - All the type contained in one inch of a typeset column.

Complete manuscript - Some editors prefer the entire written article rather than a query letter.

Composition - Typesetting which can be done by machine or hand.

Contributor's copies - Copies of the issue of a magazine sent to an author in which his or her work appears.

Copy - Manuscript material before it is set in type.

Copy editing - Editing the manuscript for grammar, punctuation and printing style as opposed to subject content.

Copyright - Usually most publications are copyrighted, meaning that the authors' works are protected from reproduction.

Correspondent - A writer away from the home office of a newspaper or magazine who regularly provides it with copy.

Cover letter - This is letter that is submitted with your complete manuscript. It should summarize your article and also remind the editor that you agreed to work on it.

Dateline - The date and place of writing an article. This is put in bold face or capital letters at the start of the first paragraph of the article; for example, Washington, DC (followed by the body of the article). The date is on the top of the page of the newspaper or magazine so it is not repeated here.

Feature article length - A lead article in the magazine. Usually it is longer.

Filler - A short item used by an editor to "fill" out a newspaper column or page in a magazine.

Free sample copy - An editor usually will send a free sample copy if the writer requests one.

Freelance writer - A writer who is not under contract for regular work but sells his writings to any buyer. The higher percentage of freelance work a publication buys, the better are the chances for the writer to sell his or her work. Also, many publications buy a lot of freelance work because they have small editorial staffs.

Ghostwriter - A writer who puts into literary form, an article, speech, story or book based on another person's ideas or knowledge.

Glossy - A black and white photograph with a shiny surface as opposed to one with a non-shiny matte finish.

Justification - The process of spacing out type to a given measure so that lines may be uniform. This is why columns in a magazine and newspaper all have the same width.

Kill fee - The writer is paid a portion of the agreed-on fee for a complete article that was assigned but which was subsequently cancelled.

Layout - The "blueprint" of a magazine that shows where copy, photos and ads go.

Market - A publication or book publishing company that is currently buying freelance material.

Measure - Width of a column of set type. The columns are all equal.

Memorandum - Once an assignment is made, an editor, in some cases, sends a letter to the writer explaining how the article should be developed, payment and deadlines. This way, both the writer and editor have a clear understanding of each other's obligations.

Model release - A paper signed by the subject of a photograph (or his guardian, if a juvenile) giving the photographer permission to use the photograph, editorially or for advertising purposes or for some specific purpose as stated.

Monthly - A magazine that comes out every month.

Ms. - Abbreviation for one manuscript.

Mss. - Abbreviation for more than one manuscript.

Multiple submissions - Some editors of non-overlapping circulation magazines such as religious publications, are willing to look at manuscripts which have also been submitted to other editors at the same time. No multiple submissions should be made to larger markets paying good prices for original material, unless it is a query on a highly topical article requiring an immediate response and that fact is so stated in your letter.

Nonfiction - Fact as opposed to inventing or making up. This is a nonfiction book.

Package sale - The editor buys a manuscript and photos as a "package" and pays the writer with one check.

Page rate - Some magazines pay for material at a fixed rate per published page, rather than so much per word.

Payment on acceptance - The writer is paid when the article is accepted, before it is published.

Payment on publication - The writer is paid after the article is published.

Pen name - The use of a name other than your legal name on articles, stories or books where you wish to remain anonymous. Simply notify your post office and bank that you are using the name so that you will receive mail and/or checks in that name.

Photo feature - A feature in which the emphasis is on the photographs rather than any accompanying written material.

Photocopies submission - Is acceptable to some editors instead of the author sending the original manuscript.

Photographer's guidelines - Guidelines a writer should follow in sending photos with a manuscript. Sometimes they are separate or included with the writer's guidelines.

Photos - Short for photographs.

Pix - This term is interchangeably used with photographs.

Proof - Impression pulled from a cut or a body of type for examination or correction.

Public domain - Material which was either never copyrighted or whose copyright term has run out.

Quarterly - A publication that comes out every quarter, three months, or four times a year.

Query - A letter to the editor to try to elicit interest in your proposed article. Always include a self-addressed, stamped envelope (SASE) with your inquiry.

Rejection slip - A letter to the writer explaining that the publication cannot use your proposed article idea. Sometimes this is a form letter.

Reporting time - The number of days and weeks it takes an editor to report back to the author on his or her query or manuscript.

Repro proofs - Proofing on special paper to assure perfect reproduction.

Rights - Writers have certain rights such as first rights and one-time rights. See the chapter in this book on "Rights and the Writer."

SASE - Abbreviation for self-addressed, stamped envelope.

Semi-monthly - A publication that comes out twice a month.

Semi-weekly - A publication that comes out twice a week.

Sidebar - A feature presented as a companion to a straight news report (or main magazine article) giving sidelights or human-interest aspects, or sometimes explaining just one aspect of the story.

Simultaneous rights - This term refers to the same article being sold simultaneously to two or more publications which do not have overlapping circulations.

Simultaneous submission - Submitting the same article to several publications at the same time.

Slant - The approach the writer should use in preparing his or her article so that it will appeal to readers of a specific magazine. See writer's guidelines for this information.

Solicited manuscript - One that is requested by the editor.

Speculation - The editor agrees to look at the author's manuscript but does not promise to buy it until he or she reads it.

Stringer - A writer who submits material to a magazine or newspaper from a specific geographical location.

Style - The way in which an article is written; for example, punchy sentences of flowing, narrative description or heavy use of quotes

Submission - The act of submitting a manuscript to an editor.

Tabloid - Newspaper format publication on about half the size of the regular newspaper page.

Tearsheet - Page from a magazine or newspaper which contains your printed article. Usually the editor will send you the entire issue. (See "contributor's copies" in this chapter).

Transparency - Positive color slide, not color print.

Uncopyrighted publication - The publication does not protect the author's work because it is not copyrighted. It is in the public domain and can, therefore, be easily reproduced.

Unsolicited manuscript - An article that an editor did not specifically ask to see.

Weekly - Comes out every week.

Writer's guidelines - Writers should follow a publication's guidelines when preparing an article. Often these guidelines will be sent for free if the writer requests them. Sometimes guidelines for submitting photographs are included. At other times, they are separate.

CHAPTER II

RIGHTS AND THE WRITER

With regard to articles, the most frequently used rights are first serial rights (or first rights), simultaneous rights, or all rights. Descriptions of each follow:

*First Serial Rights. The word serial does not mean publication in installments, but refers to the fact that libraries call periodicals "serials" because they are published in serial or continuing fashion. First serial rights means the writer offers the newspaper or magazine (both of which are periodicals) the right to publish the article, story or poem the first time in the periodical. All other rights to the material belong to the writer. Variations on this right are, for example, First North American serial rights.

*Simultaneous Rights. This term covers articles and stories which are sold to publications (primarily religious magazines) which do not have overlapping circulations. A Catholic publication editor, for example, might be willing to buy Simultaneous Rights to a Christmas story which he/she likes very much, even though he/she knows a Presbyterian magazine may be publishing the same story in one of its Christmas issues. Publications which will buy simultaneous rights indicate this fact in their listings in the writer's guidelines. Always advise an editor when the material you are sending is a simultaneous submission.

*All Rights. Some magazines, either because of the top

prices they pay for material, or the fact that they have book publishing interests or foreign magazine connections, buy All Rights. A writer who sells an article to a magazine under these terms forfeits the right to use his/her material in its present form elsewhere himself/herself. Ask the editor whether he/she is willing to buy only first rights instead of all rights before you agree to an assignment or a sale. Some editors will reassign rights to a writer after a given period-- say, one year. It is worth an inquiry in writing.

As a writer, you should strive to keep as many rights to your work as you can from the outset, because before you can resell any piece of writing, you must own the rights to negotiate. If you have sold "all rights" to an article, for instance, it can be reprinted *without* your permission, and *without* additional payment to you. Therefore, what an editor buys will determine whether you can resell your own work.

I would now like to discuss the copyright law which became effective January 1, 1978. It protects your writing, unequivocally recognizes the creator of the work as its owner, and grants the author all the rights, benefits and privileges that ownership entails. In other words, the moment you finish an article--the law recognizes that only you can decide how it is to be used.

If you look at the front page of any magazine, you will notice that the publication is copyrighted. This is the copyright symbol ( ). Personally, I would not send any material to an uncopyrighted publication. I feel that your work would not be protected.

If you look at the beginning of this book, you will notice that I own the copyright.

The following are some of the most frequently asked questions about the copyright law and how a writer can copyright an article(s) if he/she wants added protection:

*To what rights am I entitled under copyright law? The law gives you, as creator of your work, the right to print, reprint and copy the work; to sell or distribute copies of the work.

*When does copyright law take effect, and how long does it last? A piece of writing is copyrighted the moment it is put to paper. Protection lasts for the life of the author plus 50 years, thus allowing your heirs to benefit from your work. For material written by two or more people, protection lasts for the life of the last survivor plus 50 years. The life-plus-

50 provision applies if the work was created or registered with the Copyright Office after January 1, 1978, when the updated copyright law took effect. The old law protected works for a 28-year term, and gave the copyright owner the option to renew the copyright for an additional 28 years at the end of that term. Works copyrighted under the old law that are in their second 28-year term automatically receive an additional 19 years of protection (for a total of 75 years). Works in their first term also receive the 19-year extension but still must be renewed when the first term ends.

If you create a work anonymously or pseudonymously, protection lasts for 100 years after the works creation, or 75 years after its publication, whichever is shorter. The life-plus-50 coverage takes effect, however, if you reveal your identity to the Copyright Office any time before the original term of protection runs out.

*Must I register my work with the Copyright Office to receive protection? No, your work is copyrighted whether or not you register it, although registration offers certain advantages. For example, you must register the work before you can bring an infringement suit to court. You can register the work after an infringement has taken place, and then take the suit to court, but registering after the fact removes certain rights from you. You can sue for actual damages (the income or other benefits lost as a result of the infringement), but you cannot sue for statutory damages and you cannot recover attorney's fees unless the work has been registered with the Copyright Office before the infringement took place. Registering before the infringement also allows you to make a stronger case when bringing the infringement to court.

If you suspect that someone might infringe on your work, register it. If you doubt that an infringement is likely (and infringements are relatively rare), you might save yourself the time and money involved in registering the material.

*I have an article I want to protect fully. How do I register it? Request the proper form from the Copyright Office. Send the completed form, a $10 registration fee, and one copy (if the work is unpublished; two if it is published) of the work to the Register of Copyrights, Library of Congress, Washington, D.C. 20559. You need not register each work individually. A group of articles can be registered simultaneously (for a single $10 fee) if they meet these requirements:

They must be assembled in orderly form (simply placing them in a notebook binder is sufficient); they must bear a single title ("Works by Chris Jones," for example); they must represent the work of one person (or one set of collaborators); and they must be the subject of a single claim to copyright. No limit is placed on the number of works that can be copyrighted in a group.

*__Where can I get more information about copyright law?__ Write the Copyright Office, Library of Congress, Washington, D.C. 20559, for a free Copyright Information Kit. Call (not collect) between 8:30 a.m. and 5:00 p.m. if you need forms for registration of a claim to copyright. The Copyright Office will answer specific questions but will not provide legal advice.

CHAPTER III

WRITER'S CLUBS/ASSOCIATIONS

The actual writing of nonfiction articles can often be a solitary pursuit. You need a place where you can exchange ideas with other writers. I suggest that you take out a membership in a writer's club/association. Check locally if there is such an organization in your city or state.

What does a writer's club/association offer?

* A place where writers can exchange ideas.
* Some offer critique and editing of your articles.
* Some have a newsletter for their members.
* Some have an annual competition where writers can submit their works.
* Some have an annual writer's conference.
* Some have a yearly dinner/banquet where writers and their guests can get together.
* Some get involved in battles over moral issues such as censorship of books. For example, the American Society of Journalists and Authors (ASTA) got involved when books such as **The Fixer** by Bernard Malamud and **Catcher In The Rye** by J. D. Salinger were taken off school shelves.
* Some establish a code of ethics and fair practices which sets forth principles of responsible and ethical behavior by both writers and editors.
* Some offer benefits and services to their members such as an exclusive referral service, confidential market information, regular meetings with editors and others in the

field, group health insurance, and a variety of discount services.

Here are the names and addresses of 29 writers' clubs/associations. They are listed alphabetically. If you are interested in a certain organization, write for detailed information. I belong to The International Women's Writing Guild, the Wisconsin Regional Writers Association, and The Wisconsin Authors and Publishers Alliance.

1. AMERICAN AUTO RACING WRITERS AND BROADCASTING ASSOCIATION, 922 North Pass Avenue, Burbank, California 91505.
2. AMERICAN MEDICAL WRITERS ASSOCIATION (AMWA), 5272 River Road, Suite 410, Bethesda, Maryland 20816.
3. AMERICAN SOCIETY OF JOURNALISTS AND AUTHORS, INC. (ASJA) 1501 Broadway, Suite 1907, New York, New York 10036.
4. THE AUTHORS LEAGUES OF AMERICA, INC., 234 West 44th Street, New York, New York 10036.
5. DOG WRITERS' ASSOCIATION OF AMERICA (DWAA), 66 North McKinley, Hamilton, Ohio 45013.
6. EDUCATION WRITERS ASSOCIATION (EWA), 1001 Connecticut Avenue, N.W., Suite 310, Washington, D.C. 20036.
7. THE FEMINIST WRITERS GUILD, P. O. Box 14055, Chicago, Illinois 60614.
8. FLORIDA FREELANCE WRITERS ASSOCIATION (FFWW), P. O. Box 9844, Fort Lauderdale, Florida 33310.
9. INDEPENDENT WRITERS OF CHICAGO (IWOC), 645 N. Michigan, Suite 1058, Chicago, Illinois 60611.
10. INTERNATIONAL BLACK WRITERS' CONFERENCE, INC. (IBWC), P. O. Box 1030, Chicago, Illinois 60690.
11. THE INTERNATIONAL WOMEN'S WRITING GUILD (IWWG), Box 810, Gracie Station, New York, New York 10028.
12. NATIONAL ASSOCIATION OF SCIENCE WRITERS, INC., P. O. Box 294, Greenlawn, New York 11740.
13. NATIONAL WRITERS CLUB (NWC), 1450 South Havana, Suite 620, Aurora, Colorado 80012.
14. NATIONAL WRITERS UNION, 13 Astor Place, Seventh Floor, New York, New York 10003.
15. NEBRASKA WRITERS GUILD, Official Writers Organization of Nebraska, 5323 Izard Street, Omaha, Nebraska 68132.

16. OREGON ASSOCIATION OF CHRISTIAN WRITERS, 2495 Maple Avenue, N.E., Salem, Oregon 97303.
17. OUTDOOR WRITERS ASSOCIATION OF AMERICA, INC. (OWAA), 2017 Cato Avenue, Suite 101, State College, Pennsylvania 16801.
18. PEN AMERICAN CENTER, 568 Broadway, New York, New York 10012.
19. POETS & WRITERS, INC., 20 West 54th Street, New York, New York 10019.
20. SAN DIEGO WRITERS/EDITORS GUILD, 1120-172 Pepper Drive, El Cajon, California 92021.
21. SOCIETY OF AMERICAN BUSINESS EDITORS AND WRITERS (SABEW), Business Journalism Program, University of Missouri, School of Journalism, P. O Box 838, Columbia, Missouri 65205.
22. SOCIETY OF AMERICAN TRAVEL WRITERS, 1120 Connecticut Avenue, N.W., Suite 940, Washington, D.C. 20036.
23. SOCIETY OF CHILDREN'S BOOK WRITERS, P. O. Box 296, Mar Vista Station, Los Angeles, California 90066.
24. SOCIETY OF SOUTHWESTERN AUTHORS, 821 North Oracle Road, No. 128, Tucson, Arizona 85704.
25. WASHINGTON INDEPENDENT WRITERS (WIW), 220 Woodward Building, 733 Fifteenth Street, N.W., Washington, D.C. 20005.
26. WOMEN WRITERS WEST (WWW), P. O. Box 1637, Santa Monica, California 90406.
27. THE WISCONSIN AUTHORS AND PUBLISHERS ALLIANCE, P. O. Box 2131, Oshkoss, Wisconsin 54903.
28. WISCONSIN REGIONAL WRITERS ASSOCIATION (WRWA), c/o Membership Chairperson, 1303 Lost Dauphin Road, De Pere, Wisconsin 54115.
29. WRITERS ALLIANCE, 9 Garden Avenue, Miller Place, New York 11764.

PART II

TECHNIQUES -- HOW TO DEVELOP, WRITE, TYPE AND MAIL YOUR ARTICLE PLUS PAYMENT FOR ARTICLES

CHAPTER IV

THE IMPORTANT QUERY LETTER

The query letter is simply a letter asking the editor if he or she would be interested in seeing your manuscript for possible publication. Most editors require that you submit a query letter before completing the manuscript. It saves both you and the editor time.

For example, if the editor is not interested in the article and tells you so by replying negatively to your query letter, you either can send the query letter to another editor or forget the idea completely. You probably will want to do the former. On the other hand, if the editor reacts favorably to your letter, he/she is giving you the go-ahead to write the article. Still he/she is not committed to publishing the article unless you signed an agreement to that effect.

Incomplete Query Letter

Date

Editor's Name
Name of Publication
Address
Dear (Name):
 I would like to submit an article on Philadelphia for possible publication. Please let me know if you are interested.

Cordially,
(Name)
(Address)
(Phone number)

What is wrong with this query letter? Mainly, the letter is incomplete -- it hardly says anything. What, then, are the elements of a good query letter?

Elements of a Good Query Letter

Here are the ten elements of a good query letter:

* Address the letter to a specific person. Find out the editor's name or the specific person who looks at queries.

*Tell the editor how you found out about the publication. This would make a good introduction.

*Mention the main subject that your manuscript will cover. Add details such as attractions, historical sights, hotels (current rates, if possible), restaurants, shops and admission fees.

*Length of article - should adhere to what the writer's guidelines have stated. Give the length you think your article will be.

*Indicate the time it will take you to complete the article.

*Tell the availability of photos and types--black/white glossies, and/or color transparencies, with their sizes.

*State if you have had any other articles published. Sometimes this may help you get the assignment.

*Ask for copies of the writer's and photographer's guidelines and the publication.

*Type your query letter single spaced on white paper, preferably one page. Make a copy for your file.

*Include a stamped, self-addressed number 10 envelope for a reply.

Example of a Good Query Letter

The following is an example of a good query letter:

_____

                                                  Date

Editor's Name
Name of Publication
Address
Dear (name):
   I read in the March issue of *The Writer* magazine that you

are interested in receiving articles for your publication (name).

I am an avid traveler and would like to submit an article on Philadelphia which I visited last summer. Philadelphia has many attractions to offer -- Independence National Historical Park, Liberty Bell, Betsy Ross House, Christ Church and Franklin Court. The article will focus on these sights.

The article should run about 800 words and would take me about three weeks to complete. I will include one black and white glossy photo (8" x 10" size) of Independence Hall.

I have a number of travel articles published in such publications as ***The Milwaukee Journal*** and ***The Grand Rapids Press*** newspapers and ***Good Reading Magazine***.

If you are interested in having me write an article on Philadelphia, please let me know. Also, send me copies of the writer's and photographer's guidelines and a sample copy of your magazine. I hope to hear from you in the very near future.

Sincerely,
(Your Signature)
Your Name (typed)
Your Address (typed)
Your Phone number (typed)

CHAPTER V

INTERVIEWING TECHNIQUES

When preparing an article, you might have the occasion to interview one or several people and incorporate that material into your article.

Say you were writing an article about the Milwaukee Bucks. You might want to interview the manager. His or her comments would give your article an interesting angle.

How To Interview

Follow these hints and your interview should be successful:

* Make an appointment with the person you want to interview. Do not just drop in.
* Be on time for the interview.
* Allow enough time for the interview so you and the person will not be rushed.
* Prepare some questions ahead of time so that your interview will proceed smoothly.
* Determine a specific angle ahead of time so your questions will flow in that direction.
* As you proceed with the interview, additional questions will be generated.
* If possible, find out some information about the person and subject ahead of time. This way, both of you will feel comfortable at the onset of the interview. It is also a good way to start the interview.
* Use a notebook or tape recorder if the person feels com-

fortable with that arrangement.
* Ask the person to repeat quotes if you think you do not have them down correctly, or, in fact, repeat any information that you did not completely understand.
* Before you leave, thank the person for taking the time to be interviewed. A follow-up thank you note is suggested.

Writing Up The Interview

I recommend that you look through your local newspaper for interviews. Read them and you will obtain a feel for how an interview should be written.

The following are some helpful suggestions for writing up the interview:
* Use as many direct quotes as possible.
* Include some indirect quotes.
* Vary the writing style -- perhaps use a direct quote, factual information and an indirect quote. Interweave your quotes with your other information to make the article more interesting.
* Instead of always using he/she said -- other words that can be used are: commented, explained, suggested, pointed out, noted, elaborated on, added, and stated.
* If the quote is several sentences long, you do not always have to put he/she said after each sentence. It is understood that the same person is speaking.
* Sometimes the person interviewed requests that you show him/her a copy of the final interview before submitting it to the editor. This way, he or she will be able to verify if the quotes are accurate. If there is time, let the person see it, although it is not required.
* Write up the interview in the past tense unless the editor requests otherwise.
* Mail a copy of the completed or published article to the person you interviewed.

Preparing For The Interview

I am a master's degree student in journalism at Marquette University. A couple of years ago I took a course titled "Practicum in International Communication" and decided to interview the public relations director of the International Institute of Wisconsin for one of my assignments. Her name was Terry Dorr. This is the list of questions I took to the interview:

1. What is the purpose of the Institute?
2. How and when did the Institute begin?
3. What services/programs does the Institute offer?
4. Are there any new programs?
5. Tell me about the ethnic dinners, cooking classes, workshops, art exhibits and tours the Institute offers.
6. Can the public participate in the ethnic dinners, cooking classes and workshops?
7. The Institute is a referral service. Tell me how many people were served and in what ways.
8. How many people are on the Institute's staff? How many members does the Institute have?
9. Tell me about the history of the Institute. Has a history been written?
10. Since the Institute sponsors the annual Holiday Folk Fair, tell me what new things will be at the fair (performers, expanded food area and other things).
11. What are your duties at the Institute?
12. How long have you worked at the Institute?
13. What are the Institute's membership rates?
14. Is there anything else you can tell me that would be newsworthy?
15. Would you please give me a tour of the Institute?

The Written Article

I interviewed Ms. Dorr for an hour at the Institute. I asked her the above questions but not necessarily in that order. I had a notebook in which I could easily record Ms. Dorr's responses. I mailed her a typed copy of the completed article which I also submitted to my teacher. The title of the article was "International Institute of Wisconsin Reaches Out To Foreign Born People: An Interview With Terry Dorr, Public Relations Director." The verbatim text of the article follows:

The International Institute of Wisconsin has recently started two new endeavors, the International Students Speakers Bureau and a program designed to assist Wisconsin businesses and industries, according to Terry Dorr, Public Relations Director. The Institute also offers immigration and naturalization services; individual services; special workshops, classes and tours; and is one of the sponsors of the Holiday Folk Fair. In its 49th year, the Institute is a non-profit agency dedicated to promoting the interests and understanding of foreign-born people. It is located at 2810 West Highland Boulevard, Milwaukee, Wisconsin.

The International Students Speakers Bureau was begun because the Institute had received a umber of requests from elementary and secondary schools, and civic and professional organizations to give presentations. Dorr said that "undergraduate and graduate students from Milwaukee colleges and universities give the presentations. Presently there are thirty different countries represented." She added that these students re more "attuned with the recent culture and often go dressed up in native garb to the presentations." The Institute received a grant from the National Association for Foreign Student Affairs in Washington, D.C. to coordinate this program.

According to Dorr, the program to assist Wisconsin businesses and industries was begun because businesspeople often come to Milwaukee from overseas for a seminar or extended business trip. This program was designed to help with such things as translating language, assisting the businesspeople with U. S. business protocol, making up business cards, and interpreting services Dorr said the Institute has "30 people they can call on to translate." The program has a one-person staff and hopefully a newsletter can be developed in the near future.

Dorr said that the International Institute provides three types of immigration and naturalization services: casework, acculturation and interpretation/translation. There are four fulltime caseworkers who primarily work with low income people from foreign countries such as Laos, China and Spain. The casework often takes a year's time and covers such areas as legal and technical assistance in immigration and naturalization matters, refugee resettlement, job training, and placement and housing assistance. The International Institute of Wisconsin is the only non-profit social service agency in Wisconsin whose counselors are accredited to represent clients before the Immigration and Naturalization Service and the Board of Immigration Appeals.

Acculturation is the process by which the culture of a particular society is instilled in a human being. With respect to acculturation, Dorr explained that Institute staff worked with other agencies to co-sponsor "a driver safety workshop and an annual Christmas party for clients and their families in 1985."

Dorr commented that the Institute provides translations of documents, certificates business letters and contracts to community agencies, businesses and courts. A language bank of translators capable of speaking 39 languages is maintained to fulfill ongoing interpretation/translation requests.

Another purpose of the Institute, according to Dorr, "is o help people learn and teach about their ethnic heritage." She said this is done through programs such as dinners, folk dancing and folk art workshops, cooking classes, art exhibits, and tours. She elaborated on dinners that were held this past year --Hmong, Danish and Slovenian The dinners are held in the first floor hall of the Institute which holds approximately 200 people. According to Dorr, people come ahead of time and cook the ethnic dinner in the Institute's kitchen. She added that the dinners "are open to the public." They are advertised in the Milwaukee newspapers and "admission costs per person are $10.00 for Institute members and $12.00 for the public."

The Institute held a number of workshops this past year. They were on Hmong ornament making, Slovenian strudel, Hindu religion and society, and Czechoslovakian cornhusk wreaths.

Dorr stated that a complete meal is prepared and eaten in the cooking classes. This past year there were classes offered on these types of cooking: Mexican, East Indian, Greek, Creole, Chinese and Italian. Dorr enrolled in the Italian cooking class on November 8. The menu items included capponatta, tortellini carbonara, spiedini, imbottiti, zabaglione and vino. Dorr commented, "I enjoyed it all!"

The Institute also coordinates at exhibits in such locations as banks. Dorr cited the "Celebrate the Children" exhibit of children's ethnic costumes and toys which was at the Marine Bank on Wisconsin Avenue this past year.

Art tours are sponsored by the Institute. An example was the all-day tour of Japanese Buddhist art at the Chicago Art Institute on August 23. Participants ate lunch at Kiyo's Japanese Restaurant.

The Individual Services of the Institute consist of English as a Second Language (ESL) classes, international visitor/student programs and volunteer services in which international visitors are provided dinner and overnight accommodations by host families, and information and referral.

According to the 1985 Annual Report, "The International

Institute is often the first place people turn for ethnic information. From recipes to international politics, the Institute was able to provide accurate information and make referrals on a timely basis." In 1985, information was provided to 18,246 telephone callers.

Dorr stated that the Institute is one of the sponsors of the Holiday Folk Fair. She said that new attractions and improvements for this year's ethnic festival are an expanded sidewalk cafe with more food and tables, hands-on demonstration workshops on Chinese arts, two minutes of free calls to anywhere in the world can be made in the Coffee House, and the World Mart where visitors can shop for gifts and souvenirs.

The Institute has 15 fulltime staff and 1,200 members, including ethnic groups, according to Dorr. She has been with the Institute for one and one-half years. Her duties include writing brochures, news releases and editing a quarterly newsletter, "Communique." With the Institute's 50th year approaching, Dorr is contemplating writing "a history of the Institute." She said that very little history has been done on the Institute.

The following is the history that has been written about the International Institute and the international institute movement The international institute movement started about the turn of the century. It came to Milwaukee in 1923 as a YWCA program to make young immigrant women feel at home. They met, they cooked together, danced together, and learned English together.

Soon, the YWCA program outgrew the place. In 1936, a separate organization was founded. The International Institute of Milwaukee County. Because this new organization was formed and there were more funds and space, services could be increased and expanded.

With the expansion, the foreign born were not the only ones who sought the services of the International Institute. Americans came, too. Eventually the name was changed to the International Institute of Wisconsin.

Why did these people come to the International Institute? Foreign born people and their descendants came for help with problems; advice on immigration such as how to become permanent U.S. residents, what procedure to follow to bring family members here, and how to work out adoption of children from other countries.

Nationality groups, people with like interests and needs from the same countries were formed, often with the help of the Institute staff. Open houses, cultural and festive events, and nationality dinners were arranged by the Institute. By attending these events, Milwaukeeans could, and did, learn, practically one-on-one, about customs, crafts and sensitivities of people whose roots were deep in the soils of a hundred or more nations from one end of the world to another.

In the 1980s, as in the 1930s, the Institute mission goes on. In the words written for a recent slide presentation: "Here in this modest but busy building, you'll find unusually vitality, philosophy and practical skills. The International Institute is designed to help preserve and share the ethnic riches of Milwaukee's people, and perhaps even more important, to help weave newcomers into the changing fabric of everyday American life."

If you want to learn about the Institute's activities, why not become a member. International Institute membership rates are: individual, $15; family, $25; senior citizen (individual or family), $15; supporting, $100; sustaining $250; and patron, $500. The address of the International Institute of Wisconsin is 2810 West Highland Boulevard, Milwaukee, Wisconsin 53208. The telephone number is (414) 933-0521.

CHAPTER VI

COMING UP WITH AN IDEA FOR AN ARTICLE

The information on markets which I have provided has most likely given you some ideas for articles.

Let me first state some generalities. You must have a great interest in the subject you plan to write about (otherwise you will not be able to arouse interest in the reader). The subject you choose to write about must be timely. For example say you want to write about Mount Vernon, George Washington's home, you can write about the history but, in addition, should include information on what is happening today. The idea you want to write about must not be too narrow or broad in scope. In both of these cases, it would be hard to write an article because you would end up with too few or too many words.

The subject you plan to write about should be fresh, not covered recently by the publication. Try to use a different angle when writing your article. Carry a notebook along with you so you can easily jot down notes about places, people and things you were impressed with, as well as important addresses and facts that may be helpful to you in developing your article.

Read Newspapers and Magazines

Another way to obtain ideas for articles is to read local and national newspapers. Read magazines such as *Newsweek,*

People and *Time* and you are sure to come up with ideas. Read books, including those on current trends and events. In order to be a good writer, you have to be a good reader.

Look To Your Family and Friends for Ideas

In the above paragraphs, I suggested that you read newspapers, magazines and books for ideas. Do not forget your family and friends. They could easily provide you with ideas or, in some cases, be the subject of your article.

20 Ideas For Articles

Here are 20 suggestions for article ideas. This list is by no means inclusive.

* Do you, a family member, or friend have an interesting hobby?

* Have you been faced with a personal tragedy--death, divorce, sick child, or loss of a job. How did you cope?

* Is there a special lake you like to fish on? What types of fish do you catch? Why not tell readers about this?

* Are you a good cook? Why not share recipes with others?

* Do you like to sew or crochet? Tell readers what you are making and how to make the items.

* Are you experienced in tuning up your car?

* Are you in your retirement years? Tell readers what you are doing to enjoy them.

* Are you a successful business person? Tell readers how you started and why you are successful.

* Do you own rental properties? How do you go about taking care of them? Most people are interested in investments.

* Is there new construction where you live? Perhaps you could tell readers about the new baseball stadium, or sports arena.

* Do you have a pet? For example, tell how you trained it. Why not provide a photo?

* Are you a gardener? Tell readers your secrets. See the chapter on home and garden markets for places where you can sell your article.

* Do you know a disabled person? Perhaps his/her story could be an inspiration if you tell it.

* If you are a bargain hunter, you may want to tell

readers where you look for bargains on such things as clothes, antiques, and furniture.

* Did you build your own house and garage? Tell readers how.
* How do you handle your children and how do they get along with you?
* Maybe you are involved in church work. Perhaps you could come up with an idea for a religious article.
* Perhaps you have a good marriage. Tell readers what you do to maintain this.
* How do you maintain your good figure, complexion and hair? Readers are waiting to hear your secrets.
* Do you get along with your boss at work? Tell readers why.

More Article Ideas

I have suggested 20 article ideas that should get you thinking. The list is endless. Look through Part III of this book for specific publications and editors who need your ideas and articles now.

CHAPTER VII

WRITING THE ARTICLE

The actual process of writing an article usually takes much work. Let us say that an editor reacts favorably to your idea and gives you the go-ahead. Here are ten suggestions to help make the writing easier:

1. Adhere closely to the word length that the publication states.
2. Put your article in the third person unless the writer's guidelines says differently.
3. Keep your article in the same tense throughout unless you definitely have to switch in places.
4. Think of a short and snappy title that will stimulate the reader to read on.
5. Write a strong lead paragraph that will encourage the reader to read on further.
6. Add details in the middle paragraphs to help keep the article moving. For example, unique attractions, admission fees and hotels with price ranges and location are some of the things that should be included in a travel article.
7. Compose an ending that sums up the article; in other words, do not leave it hanging.
8. Make sure spelling, grammar and punctuation are correct. Keep *Webster's Dictionary* at your side.
9. Reread the article over several times before mailing it to make sure that it has continuity and says what you wanted it to say.

10. Make sure all information in the article is accurate. Double check admission fees, hotel rates, people's names and quotes.

Writing Approaches

There are many writing approaches. In this chapter, I will discuss five approaches with samples of my published works. They are:
* Informative
* Centering the article around a person
* An article using quotes
* Historical
* How to

Informative Approach

This type of article informs the reader. For example, it could include such things as the dates, times, fee, phone number, and name of the instructor. A few years ago, I taught a travel writing workshop and a short article was written about it in *The UWM Report*, a faculty/staff newsletter at the University of Wisconsin-Milwaukee where I work. The date of the newsletter was April 14, 1981.

The verbatim text of the article is as follows:

Writing Workshop Offered in May

A Travel Writing Workshop, sponsored by the Division of Urban Outreach, will be offered on three consecutive Saturday mornings: May 2, 9, and 16.

Workshop instructor, Ruth Wucherer, a freelance writer and program assistant in the UWM School of Education, will discuss travel writing markets during the first session. The class will visit the Milwaukee Public Museum during the second session, and articles written on the museum will be critiqued at the third session.

Fee for the workshop is $45. For more information, call 963-4999.

Centering The Article Around A Person

I had an article titled, "Hershey, Pennsylvania: Chocolate Capital of the World," published in *Accent*, a travel-oriented publication. I thought about the approach I would use and decided to do some research on Milton Hershey, the inventor of the famous chocolate bar. A major part of the article is devoted to Hershey and the other part deals with the attractions at the Visitor Center and Hershey Park. Two photos accompanied the text, one of Hershey and the other of equipment for chocolate production. The article was published in 1978.

Verbatim Text of Hershey Article

Following is the verbatim text of the entire article which was relatively short (about 365 words) but with the photos, it filled up one magazine page nicely.

Hershey is a place where one can enjoy eating and learning about chocolate bars and candy kisses.

The Hershey complex consists of a visitor center, plant and park. It is located eight miles north of the Pennsylvania Turnpike.

Before June 30, 1973, visitors toured the plant to find out the secrets of how the delicious Hershey chocolate products are made. But the plant tour was discontinued and replaced by the visitor center, 'Hershey's Chocolate World.'

In the center, visitors board a free automated ride which conveys them over 1,200 feet of track, past 25 scenes illustrating the story of chocolate -- from the growing and harvesting of cocoa beans in the tropics through the basic steps in the production of chocolate at Hershey's famous plant.

Children will enjoy Hershey Park, which has numerous rides and an animal contact area. The entrance to the park is Tudor Square, a 17th century English setting with a castle.

Milton Snavely Hershey was the man behind the original Hershey products. Born in Derry Township in 1857, he quit school at the age of 15 to become a printer's apprentice. Hershey did not like this type of work and switched to being a candymaker's apprentice. He worked in various parts of the country.

Then he started a caramel business which was unsuccessful at first.

After attending the Chicago Exposition in 1893, Hershey became convinced that caramels were only a 'fad,' and that chocolate would be the basis for a new industry. In 1900, he sold his caramel business and purchased chocolate-manufacturing equipment from Germany.

The chocolate business grew and Hershey decided to move

his business from Lancaster to Derry Church, which was renamed Hershey in 1906.

After much experimentation, Hershey developed his own formula for making his original milk chocolate bar. The decision to mass produce this single product, rather than continue with all different chocolate novelties, proved to be a huge success. By 1971, Hershey had $350 million in sales. Visitors can purchase the candy bars and other chocolate confections in 'Hershey's Chocolate World.'

An Article Using Quotes

At one time, I did a number of freelance articles which were published in *The Foreman's Letter*, a semi-monthly newsletter published by the National Foremen's Institute in Waterford, Connecticut. The newsletter is in existence today. I interviewed Gwendolyne Deouin who was the first woman supervisor at the Louis Allis Co. in Milwaukee, Wisconsin, and wrote this article. The article had a photo of Mrs. Derouin and was dated March 30, 1978.

The verbatim text follows:

First Female Boss Wins Respect

Gwendolyne Derouin did secretarial work for nine years and then dispatching for one year before she became the first female ever to serve as manufacturing supervisor at the Louis Allis Co., Milwaukee, Wisconsin, manufacturer of electric motors.

Mrs. Derouin, a supervisor since 1976, said she became bored with secretarial work and realized she could not advance further with it. She decided to try out for a supervisory opening and was chosen over a number of other candidates.

Now she supervises 35 first-shift workers, both men and women, in the Small Winding Department, and is one of 40 manufacturing supervisors for the company.

Mrs. Derouin says it took some time for her workers to get used to her. There were some remarks by male workers, like, 'Now I have two bosses -- one at work and one at home -- and both of them are women.'

Now, she says, everyone in the department has accepted her as the boss, and she gets full cooperation from other supervisors who are on her level.

'Sometimes it's difficult when I have a problem, because I

have no other woman on my level to relate my problems to,' says Derouin.

She says that she is very firm about job attendance:

'I feel that if I have to be here, so do my workers. I don't want part-timers. I give them a warning notice if they don't cooperate.'

She recalled one young man who had posed an absentee problem for three years. After she became his supervisor, she closely monitored his attendance weekly. He has shown continuous improvement, she says.

Historical

Another approach when writing an article is the historical approach. In this type of article, you write about the history of a place and stress some dates. At the same time, you tell the reader about what is happening today. My article on Greenfield Village, with one photo, was published on the travel page of *The Grand Rapids Press* newspaper. I like the way the editor highlighted a couple of paragraphs by printing them in bold face. The date of the article was August 13, 1984.

The verbatim text of the article follows:

Greenfield Village Offers 300 Years of U.S. History
By Ruth Wucherer

DEARBORN - Covering 300 years in a day is a neat trick.

One can try it with a visit to the Henry Ford Museum and Greenfield Village.

That's where three centuries of American life -- through the development of arts and skills -- is capsuled on the 14 acres of the museum and its neighbor, the 240-acre village.

Of course, you have to move fast when looking over the 250,000 objects in the museum and the 85 buildings in the village. And it may take the visitor more than a day to see everything in the Edison Institute (the name of the museum and village since it was founded as a non-profit educational institution in 1929).

The automobile, of course, is one of the big attractions here. There are about 180 on display in the Henry Ford Museum Automobile Collection in the Hall of Technology. The exhibit's period spans the years 1865 to 1959.

An 1865 Roper, a steam carriage built by Sylvester Hayward Roper in Roxbury, Massachusetts, was acquired by Henry Ford in 1930.

On the second floor of the museum is a Ford Quadricycle, which is a replica of the first car made by Ford. A 1903 Ford Model A, the first car Ford offered for public sale, and a 1909 Ford Model T also are in the collection.

Other oldies in the museum are a 1903 Oldsmobile, 1903 Packard, 1915 Cadillac, 1916 Mercer Touring car an 1923 Chevrolet.

Those who may want a change from old autos will find a huge collection of musical instruments in the Music and Decorative Arts Galleries of the museum. Ford purchased, in 1928, the Daniel S. Pillsbury Collection of 155 brass instruments, 14 woodwind instruments and six percussion instruments from the 19th century.

The development of office machines, printing, radio, telegraphy, telephones, television, microwave and wireless telegraphy is included in the interesting Communications Collection in the museum.

The museum and village also contain other collections such as bicycles, camping vehicles, commercial vehicles, fire apparatus, aircraft, railroad equipment and artifacts associated with U.S. presidents.

The Agricultural Collection is one of the most comprehensive in the nation. It includes the first iron plow.

Greenfield Village surrounds the museum and shouldn't be missed, for it traces life in the U.S. from the 17th to 20th centuries.

Ford didn't forget his friend, Thomas Alva Edison, in the village. The Edison West Orange Laboratory, where Edison invented the first successful incandescent lightbulb, is there.

Visitors can also see the courthouse where Abraham Lincoln once practiced law, the house where Noah Webster compiled his dictionary and the shop where Orville and Wilbur Wright built the first components of their original airplane.

Demonstrations in the Village Crafts Center feature bread and cookie baking, candle dipping, glass blowing, leatherwork, pottery and printing.

The transition from an agricultural to an industrial society is illustrated in the seven factories, shops and mills in the Village Industrial Area. Included are the Harahan Sugar Mill, Stony Creek Sawmill, Armington and Sims Machine Shop,

Richard Carriage Shop, and Macon Brick Works.

As for accommodations, there are a number of restaurants on the grounds and a free brochure, 'Henry Ford Museum and Greenfield Village Hotel, Motel and Campground Packages,' is available by writing to the Edison Institute, Henry Ford Museum and Greenfield Village, P. O. Box 1970, Dearborn, Michigan 48121.

It is about a three-hour drive from the Grand Rapids area so take that into consideration because hours are 9 a.m. to 5 p.m. daily with the exception of Thanksgiving, Christmas and New Year's days.

Museum admission prices are: adults, $8; children 6 through 12, $4; children under 6, free; and senior citizens, $7; with group rates available.

Village admission prices are: adults, $8; children 6 through 12, $4; children under 6, free; senior citizens, $7; groups rates are available. A two-day (consecutive) unlimited admission ticket to the museum and village is available for $14 to adults, $6 to children 6 through 12, and $12 to senior citizens.

How-to Approach

I have not written any how-to articles but I have written a how-to book. In this type of article or book, you give detailed instructions on how to do something. I authored a book which tells how to write travel articles and get them published. It is titled, *Travel Writing For Fun & Profit: How To Add Dollars To Your Income Writing Travel Articles and Getting Them Published.* The publisher is R&E Publishers, the publisher of this book. You can order a copy of the book from R&E Publishers, P. O. Box 2008, Saratoga, California 95070. The cost is $9.95 plus an additional charge for shipping and handling.

This is the description of my book which appeared in the brochure on books published by R&E Publishers:

"Have you ever thought about writing on your travels and submitting the article to a travel publication with the hopes of getting it published? This book, *Travel Writing For Fun and Profit*, offers you valuable suggestions on how to accomplish this. You will be proud that your work was published and add dollars to your income at the same time.

This book contains 16 chapters with such headings as, 'The Travel Writer's Vocabulary,' 'Coming Up With An Idea For A

Travel Article,' 'Interviewing Techniques,' 'The Important Query Letter,' 'Writing The Article,' and 'Photos Will Help To Sell Your Article.'

The first three chapters list markets that are presently interested in receiving travel articles. These 30 golden opportunities include travel publications, automobile and travel club magazines, recreational vehicle and camping publications, inflight magazines and others. Current information on the specific types of articles needed, word length, rate of payment, whom to send the article to, and submission of photos are covered. The author personally wrote each publication to obtain the most updated information.

Ruth Wucherer, the author, has had various travel articles published in such publications as *Accent* magazine, *The Milwaukee Journal* newspaper and others. She has also authored one book on selling crafts, three booklets, and feature and business articles. A goldmine of good ideas to get started and be successful.

Summary

The material in this chapter covered several writing approaches that one could possibly use in developing an article. There are other approaches; in fact, invent your own. Strive for uniqueness and interest in your article -- that in turn should make the editor want to buy it.

If the article is published, do not feel bad if the editor changes the title or wording of the article or even shortens it. These are usually done because of space requirements.

CHAPTER VIII

TYPING AND MAILING YOUR ARTICLE

I usually do several drafts of my article before I do the final draft. I write out the first draft in longhand. I type succeeding drafts until I feel the article is perfect.

One thing that you want to accomplish when typing your manuscript is to make it look professional. If you want an editor to even consider your manuscript, make sure that it is neatly typed, that the typewritten copy is not blotted by coffee stains, and that the manuscript is not crumbled.

It goes without saying that your typewriter should be clean, and your ribbon new. Your manuscript should be typewritten and not submitted in longhand. If you do not know how to type, ask or hire someone else to do the job.

Now the job of typing the manuscript begins. Here are twelve suggestions to make the task easier:

1. Make a carbon copy of your manuscript. This way if it gets lost, you will have a copy.
2. If you are using a computer, make a xerox copy for yourself.
3. Type your name in the lefthand corner of each page.
4. Insert the title in capital letters in the center of the first page about a third of the way down.
5. Double space your manuscript throughout unless the writer's guidelines have told you differently.
6. Use 8-1/2" x 11" size white bond paper.
7. Erase errors neatly. I use correction tape. I do not

correct the carbon copy. If there are too many errors on one page, I retype it.

8. Put the word count on the first page in the upper righthand corner.

9. Leave adequate margins of at least 1-1/2" on all four sides, except on the first page. This will give the editor room to write notes in the margin; for example, notes to the printer.

10. Type each line regularly across the page. You do not have to type your copy into columns; the printer will take care of this.

11. On the second page, again type your name in the lefthand corner and on the second line, put "Add One" (plus key word of title of article). Do this on successive pages but put "Add Two", "Add Three", etc.

12. Put the word "more" on the bottom of each page (centered) until you get to the end of the article where you should put "-0-" (centered).

This page and the next page show outlines of how the first, succeeding, and last pages of your article should look.

Outline of Page One of Article

Ruth Wucherer   Article Word Count

Start the article 1/3 of the page down

Greenfield Village Offers
300 Years of U.S. History

___

1-1/2" margin   1-1/2" margin

body of article

double space copy
and
indent each paragraph five spaces

more
(Write more to indicate that more
follows on next page)

___

1-1/2" margin

Outline of Succeeding Pages of Article

Ruth Wucherer
Add One Greenfield Village

1-1/2" margin
_____

1-1/2" margin   Continuation of article   1-1/2" margin

more
_____
1-1/2" margin

Last Page of Article

Ruth Wucherer
Add Five Greenfield Village

1-1/2" margin
_____

1-1/2" margin   end of article
-0-   1-1/2" margin
_____
1-1/2" margin

Cover Letter

Instead of just sending your manuscript to the editor, include a cover letter. This is a good way to remind the editor that you have completed the article and also is an opportunity for you to express your hope that it will be published in the near future. Also state if you are including photos with the manuscript.

The cover letter should be short, no more than one typewritten page. It might read as follows:

                                                            Date
Editor's Name
Publication's Name
Address

Dear Editor (name):
  Enclosed find an article and three black and white photos of Greenfield Village and the Henry Ford Museum in Dearborn, Michigan.
  About a month ago, I wrote you a query letter saying that I would like to submit an article on this subject. You told me to go ahead.
  I hope that this material is acceptable and that it will be published in the very near future. If it is published, please send me complimentary copies of the article.

                                                     Cordially,
                                                     Ruth Wucherer
                                                     (address)
                                                     (phone #)
Enclosures

  If you have not heard anything from the editor about your article within a month, you should inquire about its status.
  When you mail your article and photos, use a manila envelope (10x13 size). Also include another envelope inside, addressed to you and with sufficient postage clipped to it, in case your article and photos are returned.
  You can mail your article and photos first class or fourth class (the manuscript rate). I always mail my material first class because articles are usually not that lengthy and I feel that the article will get there faster.
  If you include photos with your manuscript, you should write "Photos Enclosed - Do Not Bend" on the outer envelope. This will alert the mail people that there are photos in the package and hopefully they will handle it with more

care and not crush it.

For added protection, you might want to insure your manuscript. Check with your local post office for rates.

I think investing in a miniature postal scale is worthwhile. This way you can weigh your own material and do not have to always make a trip to the post office.

If you have a large manuscript and numerous photos, you may want to put your materials in a jiffy bag rather than a manila envelope. Jiffy bags provide better cushioning. The jiffy bags and postal scale can be purchased at an office supply store or discount store such as K-Mart or Target.

Article Critique Checklist

Here are 20 points to check yourself on when writing, typing and mailing your manuscript and submitting photos:

1. Have I requested several copies of the publication I am considering submitting an article to and have I read them thoroughly to get a feel for the style and contents? Often the editor will send the copies for free.

2. Have I queried the editor about my idea unless it says to send the finished manuscript? Have I included a stamped, self-addressed envelope for a reply?

3. The article should be geared towards a specific market. For example, if the publication wants articles on the Eastern United States, do not send material on the Midwest. Also follow the article length that is specified.

4. Is the subject matter broad enough so an article can be easily written? Still it should not be too broad because then the article would never end.

5. Does the article have a specific angle? For example, it may focus on a certain person, anniversary, or attraction. Avoid the familiar.

6. It is best to write the article in the third person unless the writer's guidelines state otherwise.

7. Admission rates, hours open, important addresses, special events, what is unique -- are some of the things that should be included in the article.

8. When you travel, carry around a notebook and take down information. Also collect brochures. This material will help you to prepare the article.

9. Remember, if you need photos, you can write directly to the places, state tourist offices or state chambers of commerce. They will often send these photos for free. Be

sure that the photos are captioned and properly credited. See the chapter in this book that covers this subject.

10. Are grammar, punctuation and spelling correct in the article?

11. Type the article on 8-1/2" x 11", white, bond paper unless other directions are specified. Put the article word count in the upper righthand corner.

12. Are the lead and end paragraphs strong? Does the article flow? Read the article over several times before mailing it out.

13. Have I used the correct typing format? Recheck the writer's guidelines.

14. Have I left adequate margins on each page?

15. Have I included an additional self-addressed, stamped envelope in case the article is returned? Is there sufficient postage on the top envelope?

16. Wait about a month for a reply on your article. Otherwise, write the editor to find out about its status.

17. Have I requested complimentary copies of the published article in my cover letter?

18. Have I typed a cover letter to go along with the article or article/photo(s)?

19. Have I made a copy of the article for myself?

20. If one editor rejects your article, do not get discouraged. Send it to another, but do not send the same article simultaneously to two or more editors unless the writer's guidelines say this is okay. It could get you into trouble and it is not good ethics.

CHAPTER IX

PHOTOS WILL HELP SELL YOUR ARTICLE

If you want to sell an article, photos will definitely help persuade the editor to buy your work. This is especially true for travel, regional, sports, hobby and craft articles. In fact some editors will not accept the article unless you supply photos. Some editors purchase the text-photo package as one and do not offer any additional payment for photos, while others offer extra payment. Read the "Photographer's Guidelines" before submitting photos to the magazine. Sometimes the photographer"s guidelines are separate or are incorporated in with the writer's guidelines. In either case, include a SASE (self-addressed, stamped envelope) when requesting the guidelines. The following 20 terms are ones with which I think a writer should be familiar.

Photo Terms

Acetate - Transparent plastic film.

B & W - Abbreviation for black and white photograph. Editors usually prefer the 8 x 10 size.

Caption - Description of the subject matter of the photograph, including names of people where appropriate. Usually this information is placed under the photo. Also called a **cutline**.

Color separation - Separating the full-color transparency into the four basic color negatives for process printing.

Contrast - The tonal gradation between highlights and

shadows.

Credit line - Giving proper credit if you have not taken the photo. The credit line is put after the caption and enclosed in parentheses.

Crop - Cutting a photo down so that it will fit the space. The publication's staff will handle this.

Glossy - A black and white photograph with a shiny surface as opposed to one with a non-shiny matte finish.

Halftone - A reproduction of a continuous tone illustration (photograph or artwork) with the image formed by camera-screened dots of various sizes.

Kodalith - High contrast film generally used in printing.

Master print - The very best darkroom result in a black and white photograph as opposed to a working print without all the refinements.

Matte finish - Dull-coated paper without gloss; some black and white photos have this finish.

Model release - A paper signed by the subject of a photograph (or his guardian, if a juvenile) giving the photographer permission to use the photograph, editorially or for advertising purposes or for some specific purpose as stated.

Photo feature - A feature in which photographs are emphasized rather than the accompanying written material.

PMT - Stands for Photo Mechanical Process, a Kodak process.

Portfolio - Folder for carrying photographic or artwork samples.

PSA - Stands for Photographic Society of America.

Slides - Usually called transparencies by editors who want color photographs.

Stock photo - Often tourist attractions and tourist offices have a selection of photos in stock that are available to writers if they request them. Usually, they will be sent to the writer for free, especially if he or she is preparing a travel article.

Transparency - Positive color slides which have a picture or design that is visible when light shines through them. Editors usually prefer these sizes: 35mm, 2-1/4" x 2-1/4", or larger.

Points To Consider When Taking Photos

If you decide to take your own photos, here are several points to consider to make them better. In addition, you

should read some photography books or attend a photography class.
* Try to have a single dominating or main point of interest. Do not overcrowd your picture with too many objects.
* Choose a background for a figure or group. This could be a doorway, clump of bushes, landscape or shoreline. This background will serve as a setting or frame for your photo.
* Equalize light and dark tones. For example, all of the dark values should not be in one place. Gradations from light to dark tones are needed.
* Let your subjects look natural, not like they are posing.
* If you are doing a series of photos, try to achieve continuity.
* Try for an unusual viewpoint. Do not hold your camera level all the time; move it up or down. Then snap-you should get a unique result.
* Obtain a three-dimension effect through a variety of lighting. This will add depth to your photo. You do not always have to have light coming from behind your photos.
* Frame your photos; this will make them less commonplace. For example, a castle could be framed by foliage and a fence.
* If you are taking a photo of a moving figure or object, move your camera in unison with it. This will avoid blurring.
* If you are taking color photos, flat and even lighting is essential. Lighting one part of your subject much more strongly than the rest will make other parts much too dark and color will be lost. This applies to the principal subject, background and foreground.

Obtaining Photos

If you feel that you would not take good photos or do not have the time, you can easily obtain photos from the tourist attraction you are writing the article about or from the state tourist office where the attraction is located Also, the state chambers of commerce may have photos.

Here is a sample letter you can send to the tourist attraction. If you send it to the Public Information Officer, it should get to the right person.

```
                                                              Date
Public Information Officer
Address


Dear Public Information Officer:
    I am writing an article on the Circle Line Cruise of New York and its boroughs. I need photographs to accompany the article. Would you please send me some glossy black and white photos (8" x 10", preferably) of the Cruise Line boat and attractions you see while taking the cruise?
    Also, I would appreciate updated information on the days, months and times the cruise is given, admission costs, and any other helpful information.
    If the article is published, I will be happy to send you a copy. I hope to hear from you in the very near future.

                                                         Sincerely
                                                        Your Name
                                                     Your Address
                                                    Your Phone No.
```

In my experience, by writing a letter like this, the public information officer would send an entire packet containing photos and information. This information is very valuable because you may not have the time to write your article immediately and this way you would have updated information.

You may not receive as high a payment for photos that you did not take. On the other hand, you may be paid the same amount as if you took your own photos. It depends on the editor.

Writing Captions

In order to obtain an idea of how to write photo captions, look through magazines and newspapers. Captions contain few words. They should capture the attention of the reader.

A number of methods can be used to type captions. For black and white photos, type the caption on a sheet of paper and tape it to the bottom of the back of the photo with masking tape. This will allow the editor to easily remove the copy for typesetting. The caption should fold over the front of the photo so that the editor can fold it back for easy reading. Another method is to type the captions on a separate sheet of paper and assign each a number corresponding with its photo. The paper can be placed before the packet of photos.

Captions for color transparencies, 2-1/4" x 2-1/4" size or larger, can be typed on thin strips of paper inserted in the acetate sleeve protecting the transparency. For 35mm transparencies, type the captions on a separate sheet and assign corresponding numbers. Color prints are not acceptable in most cases.

Each black and white photograph should carry your name and address on the back and some identifying number (written lightly on the back of the photo in pencil, so as not to damage the photo surface itself).

For color transparencies, your name and address, and some picture identification can be placed on the small mounts; the rest can be typed on a separate sheet. The transparencies, each in a transparent protective sleeve, can be hinged with tape to the top of the caption sheet.

Model Release

Some magazines and newspapers require model releases from photographed people. A model release is required of all recognizable persons in a picture which is to be used for advertising purposes (including photographs appearing on a magazine cover, in sponsored publications and company brochures). The release is used, for example, if you actually appeared in the photo, or if someone else did. There is a possibility that you could be in one of your photos accompanying your article if someone else took your photo.

The release protects the photographer against possible suits for invasion of privacy or legal damages, since many states have laws which forbid a name, picture or quotation from being used for commercial purposes without the subject's authorization.

If the person in the photograph is a minor, the release must be signed by his or her parents or guardians.

Never send your original model release along with a photograph. Instead, send a copy and keep the original in your file.

A sample model release could read this way:

"In consideration for value received, receipt whereof is acknowledged, I (your name) hereby give (name of film or publication) the absolute right and permission to copyright and/or publish, and/or re-sell photographic portraits or pictures of me, or in which I may be included in whole or in part, for art, advertising, trade or any other lawful purpose whatsoever.

I (your name) hereby waive any right that I may have to inspect and/or approve the finished product or the advertising copy that may be used in connection therewith, or the use to which it may be applied.

I (your name) release, discharge and agree to save (name of firm or publication) from any liability by virtue of any blurring, distortion, alteration, optical illusion or use in composite form, whether intentional or otherwise, that may occur or be produced in the making of said pictures, or in any processing tending towards the completion of the finished product.

Signature_____   Model_____
Date_____   Address_____
Witness_____

Packing Photos

Here are some helpful hints for packing photos:

* If you typed your captions on a separate sheet(s), put this sheet first before the photographs.
* Pick up corrugated cardboard inserts from your local grocery store.
* Place your black and white photos between two corrugated cardboard inserts, wrap two rubber bands around them, and mail the photos with your manuscript in a 9" x 12" or 10" x 13" size envelope. If you have numerous photos, you may want to pack them separately from your manuscript.
* To mail transparencies, use slotted acetate sheets, which hold twenty slides and offer protection from scratches, moisture, dirt and dust. These acetate sheets are available in standard sizes from most photo supply houses. Do not use glass mounts. Mail the transparencies like you would black and white photos.

*   Because transparencies are irreplaceable (unless you have negatives or duplicates made), be sure to insure them.
*   Print "PHOTOS ENCLOSED - DO NOT BEND" on the outer mailing envelope.
*   Enclose a self-addressed, stamped envelope in case your materials would be returned. Be sure that postage is sufficient for both the photos and manuscript. You can attach the stamps to the inner envelope with a paper clip or in a separate small envelope. This way if your materials are not returned, the editor could send you back the postage. Usually, though, they keep it. One outer envelope and one inner envelope (folded - same size) are usually enough unless you have a thick manuscript and numerous photos to mail. If you have a thick manuscript and numerous photos, mail the manuscript and photos in separate envelopes with sufficient return postage.

CHAPTER X

PAYMENT FOR ARTICLES KEEPING TRACK OF SALES AND EXPENSES

After you have written your article and submitted it to the editor, you may ask, "When do I receive the check?" It may be awhile because most publications do not pay until the article is published. This may be a few months off. A few publications pay when the article is accepted. A few also offer a kill fee where the writer gets paid a certain fee even if the article is not published.

I would not recommend sending an article to a publication that pays less than $.10 a word. I just do not think it is worth it. Although that is a personal opinion. You can work with lower paying markets in the beginning, then gradually work up to higher paying ones.

The amount a writer gets paid for an article is usually listed on the writer's and photographer's guidelines. If you have sold several articles to the same editor, you may receive more compensation as time goes on.

One thing that should not discourage a writer is if the editor cuts his/her original manuscript because of space limitations. This is a common practice. Usually the editor will not tell the writer ahead of time; the writer first finds out when he or she sees the final published article. Sometimes, though, the editor does not cut the article. The editor should send you several copies of the issue in which your work is published. If not, you should request them.

If a writer feels that the article has been substantially changed by the cuts, he or she has a right to complain to the editor. A writer only gets paid for the words that were actually published.

Non-Payment for Articles

Perhaps an editor does not pay you at all for an article. What can you do in this case? First, you could mention it to the editor and hope that he or she will pay you. Second, you could hire a lawyer. But in most cases this is not feasible because your article payment would not be that high. If you do not succeed in getting paid, I would never work with the editor again.

Freelance Writer's Agreement

Most editors do not give a writer a freelance writer's agreement to sign because most first articles are written on speculation. If a writer has written several articles for a publication that were accepted, he or she most likely will be asked to sign an agreement. The agreement covers such areas as how the article should be written, payment rate schedule and reimbursement for telephone calls.

Here is a sample freelance writer's agreement from Brentwood Publishing Corp. which publishes *Association & Society Manager* and *Incentive Travel Manager* magazines. The agreement is reprinted with the permission of Brentwood Publishing Corp., a Prentice-Hall/Simon & Schuster unit of Gulf + Western, Inc.

Freelance Writer's Agreement
Brentwood Publishing Corp.
1640 Fifth Street
Santa Monica, California 90401

In connection with the various articles which we may assign to you as free-lance writer, you have agreed to abide by our rules and regulations as herein set forth with reference to all assignments you accept.

*You must record all telephone interviews and turn in the tapes to us along with your article. You will notify the person being interviewed that the telephone interview is being recorded and abide by all of the laws regarding recording of telephone interviews.

*You are to rework the verbatim statements from the transcriptions of the taped interview, organizing and clarifying all statements for incorporation into the finished article as quotes. In doing so, you shall retain the meaning of the verbatim quotes and not take the quotes out of context so as to change the meaning the person interviewed intended to convey to you.

*You are responsible for complete accuracy of quotes, spelling of name, title, and affiliation of person interviewed. You must also follow our "red dot" policy. The first time a person's name and title appears in the article, please put a red dot over it to verify the spelling.

*You are to submit the article with correct basic sentence structure, grammar, spelling, and punctuation. Repeated errors in basic writing skills will be a cause for rejection of the article for any reason whatsoever. Should we reject the article, which we retain the right to do at our sole discretion, no payment will be made to you for such article. It is understood and agreed that you are to be paid only for those articles which we accept.

*You must furnish a directory of participants with your article which states the name, title, affiliation, address, and phone number of each person interviewed.

For all of your articles that we accept, you are to be paid in accordance with the quoted rate schedule attached hereto no later than thirty (30) days after our acceptance of your article.

You understand and agree that you will not be paid for any articles which we do not accept, and we reserve the right to cancel any assignment at any time without any obligation to pay you for any work you may have done prior to our cancellation of your assignment.

Rate schedule:

In addition to the fee to be paid you for accepted articles, we agree to reimburse you for all telephone expenses incurred by you in connection with such articles not to exceed One Hundred Fifty Dollars ($150) per article. You will not be reimbursed for any telephone expense in excess of $150 per article unless you have first obtained our written consent. Payment for your telephone expense, however, is contingent upon your submitting to us a log sheet setting forth the information as to all calls made in connection with each article, showing date of the call, person called, and telephone number, which log sheet shall be certified by you as being correct. Also, you shall furnish us with the original or a photocopy of your telephone bill, indicating thereon the calls made for each article. The information on the log sheet and on the telephone bill must be consistent. You shall be reimbursed for such telephone expense no later than two (2) weeks after our receipt of your certified log and telephone bill.

We will reimburse you for your telephone expenses incurred in connection with these assignments whether the article is accepted or rejected; provided, however, that you submit a bona fide draft of the article to us on or before the deadline on the assignment sheet. You are expected to submit to us all articles by the deadline given to you at the time of the assignment, and we will not reimburse you for any telephone expense if you make calls and subsequently decide not to write the article, or if you fail to submit the article on or before the deadline on the assignment sheet.

It is understood that we are under no obligation to assign any articles to you nor are you under any obligation to accept assignments from us.

You shall not assign your rights or delegate performance of your duties as a free-lance writer for us without our prior written consent.

It is understood and agreed that all proprietary rights to articles you write for this company, for which you are paid in full, belong to Brentwood Publishing Corp., and you have no patent right or copyright equity whatsoever in the material and/or subject matter of said material which is purchased from you by Brentwood Publishing Corp.

It is further understood and agreed that you are not an agent or legal representative of our company for any purpose whatsoever, and you do not have any right or authority to assume or to create any obligation or responsibility in behalf of or in our name or to bind our company in any manner whatsoever.

You further agree to keep all information received from us confidential, and you agree not to use any such information directly or indirectly in any manner whatsoever, except in connection with any articles prepared for us.

If the foregoing arrangement is satisfactory with you,

please sign and return this agreement.

I have read the above information and agree to each and all of the terms and conditions thereof and agree to accept freelance writing assignments from Brentwood Publishing Corp. solely on the terms and conditions set forth above.

NAME	(type or print)	
SIGNATURE		DATE
ADDRESS		
CITY	STATE	ZIP
PHONE	(home)	(office)

Keeping Track of Sales

If you have sold one article in a year, you probably will not want to report it on your yearly federal and state tax forms. It would not be worth all the effort.

On the other hand, let us say that you have had some sales. It is a good idea to get into the practice of keeping track of your sales and expenses. Besides article sales, include fees for workshops and speaking engagements (if appropriate). I have done some of the latter. When I record the entries, I put the date I received the check, the title of the article, the publication in which it appeared, and the amount of the check. Here are samples of my entries:

Writing Sales and Fees for 1987

Date	Title & Name of Publication	Amount
8/9	Washington, D.C.'s Great Museums Good Reading Magazine	$ 50.00
11-10	History Comes Alive in this City (Philadelphia) - The Grand Rapids Press Newspaper	$ 90.00
12/15	Taught Travel Writing Class (6 sessions) at Marquette Univ.	$400.00
	TOTAL	$540.00

After you list all your article sales, teaching of classes and speaking engagements, calculate the total.

Keeping Track of Expenses

Keep track of your writing expenses the same way you keep track of your writing sales. Here is how your expense sheet might look.

1987 Writing Business Expenses

Date	Type of Expense	Amount
1/7	3 Year Subscription to Writer's Digest Magazine (at special rate)	$ 37.00
2/15	5 Reams of Typing Paper	$ 5.00
3/10	100 ($.22) Stamps	$ 22.00
	TOTAL	$ 64.00

Again, total your expenses. Other expenses you should keep track of are telephone (local and long distance calls), computer and computer supplies, and office space. I would recommend that you talk to someone who is knowledgeable about taxes so you know what you can deduct. This person will also tell you the proper forms to use if you want to report your sales and expenses.

PART III

THE MARKETS --

OVER 150 PLACES (12 DIFFERENT CATEGORIES) TO SELL YOUR WORK, PLUS SAMPLES OF MY PUBLISHED WORKS

CHAPTER XI

GENERAL INTEREST PUBLICATIONS

General interest publication editors are interested in receiving freelance material. What is a general interest publication? It is a publication that appeals to the general public. There are a variety of articles in these publications. Travel nature, sports and personal achievement are examples.

An example of a general interest publication is *Good Reading*, a monthly magazine published by The Henry F. Henrichs Publications, Inc., Litchfield, Illinois 62056. It is a handy size, 5-1/4" x 7-1/4", with 32 pages.

My article, "Washington, D.C.'s Great Museums," appeared in the August 1984 issue of *Good Reading* magazine. Besides my article, there were other articles with these titles-- "Quebec '84, a fete internationale," "Thank You, Mr. Hershey," "Views of a Vanishing Frontier," "Motivation," "The Ringling Brothers Centennial," "A Look at Old Ste. Genevieve" and "Anonymous' Greatest Works." Regular features were "Youth Today," "Easy Does It," "In the Sportlite," "Notes and Notions," "Random Reflections," "Tales to Tell Again," "Would You Believe It!" and "After All."

My article appeared on pages 5 and 6. The verbatim text of the article follows:

Washington, D.C.'s
GREAT MUSEUMS
by Ruth Wucherer

Flying machines and spacecraft, realistic portraits, American art and African art ... the Smithsonian Institution museums have something for everyone. What makes them even more appealing is they can be seen for free. There are 13 museums and a zoological park, including the National Air and Space Museum (attracting a daily average of 50,000 visitors), Hirschorn Museum and Sculpture Garden and The National Portrait Gallery.

The Air and Space Museum has 23 exhibit galleries focusing on such subjects as milestones of flight, air transportation, vertical flight, jet aviation and flight testing. The newest gallery, "Golden Age of Flight" features planes, personalities and aviation events that marked the years between the two world wars.

The cobalt-blue flight suit of Sally K. Ride was recently unveiled at the museum. The suit is an addition to the exhibit entitled "America's Space Truck--the Space Shuttle," located in the museum's Space Hall. Ride, who was the first American woman in space, was a member of the Challenger space shuttle team mission in June, 1983.

Tourists can learn about space and related subjects from theater films. A new film in the Albert Einstein Spacearium, "The Oldest Dream: A Celebration of Flight." recalls the major triumphs and setbacks in flight. Also, the Samuel P. Langley Theater features such films as "Hail Columbia!," "Living Planet," "To Fly" and "Flyers."

Air Express -- the shipping of packages by air overnight-- is the subject of a new exhibit in the museum's Hall of Air Transportation. "Air Express--New Life to an Old Idea" features models, photographs and a film, with a Dassault Cargo Falcon Jet as the centerpiece.

Next to the National Air and Space Museum is the Hirshhorn Museum and Sculpture Garden, focusing on modern art and sculpture. Opened in 1974, it is named after the man who donated his art collection to it, Joseph H. Hirshhorn (1899-1981).

Especially impressive is Larry River's colorful, 33-foot-long assemblage, The History of the Russian Revolution from Marx to Mayakovsky, on the second floor. In addition, the museum displays 2,500 works on paper ranging from drawings, prints, watercolors and gouaches dating from the late 19th century to the present. Works of both American and European artists are represented.

Exhibits frequently change at the Hirshhorn Museum. Until August 19, 1984, an exhibit focusing on works done by two or more individuals will be on display. Approximately 90 collaborative works will range from paintings, sculptures, collages, photographs and prints, as well as kinetic, video and conceptual pieces. The largest sculpture in the exterior plaza is Isis by Mark di Suvero. It stands 42 feet high and weighs 30 tons.

Nearby is another Smithsonian museum, The National Portrait Gallery. Tourists should not miss the Hall of Presidents on the second floor. Decorated in the grand style of the mid-nineteenth century, the Hall features portraits and associative items describing the public and private lives of our Chief Executives. On the same floor, tourists can become acquainted with Civil and post-Civil War America as recorded in the vast J. Frederick Hill Reserve Collections. The outstanding piece in this collection is the famous "cracked plate" negative of Alexander Gardner's likeness of Abraham Lincoln, taken just four days before his assassination.

Seven Smithsonian Institution museums are located on the National Mall between the Washington Monument and the Capitol. Five other museums and the National Zoological Park are located elsewhere in Washington. The only Smithsonian outside of Washington is the Cooper-Hewitt Museum in New York City.

The names of the other Smithsonian Institution museums in Washington are: Freer Gallery of Art, National Gallery of Art, National Museum of American History, National Museum of Natural History, National Museum of American Art, Arts and Industries Building, Renwick Gallery, Museum of African Art and Anacostia Neighborhood Museum. The administrative building, popularly known as the Castle, houses the visitor information center.

-end-

My comments on the above article are:
1. Free admission is stressed. Emphasize this in an article if this is true.
2. There are 13 museums and a zoological park but this article focused on three museums. Because of space requirements, I could only write on a certain number of museums.
3. The length of the article is short, about 900 words. This is about average for a magazine article. Usually articles are longer.

4. A black and white photo of The National Portrait Gallery was included with the article. Photos often help to sell an article.

5. In the last two paragraphs, I included information on names and locations of the other Smithsonian museums. This is a good way to end the article.

6. The article appeared in the August issue which I felt was very good because many tourists visit the Smithsonians in the summer months.

I did not get paid that much for this article, $50 if I recall correctly, but I liked the way *Good Reading* editors handled it. I also was proud of the fact that the article appeared near the front of the magazine.

Good Reading Editorial Requirements

Good Reading editors are looking for a variety of nonfiction articles: business, success and personal achievement, humorous, nature, inventions and crafts, travel (foreign and domestic), and biography (current and historical). Seasonal material is also welcome. Maximum word length is 1,000 words. Good quality, b/w glossy photos should accompany the article. There is no additional payment for photos. Payment for articles is $20 to $100. Cartoons, short quizzes and puzzles are purchased for $10 apiece. Payment is made on acceptance of the material and *Good Reading* purchases First North American serial rights with the privilege of reprinting the material in any of the Sunshine Press publications. ***Send the complete article, cartoon, quiz or puzzle; do not query***. Sample copies of *Good Reading* magazine are available on request at $.50 each (include a SASE). Send material to *Good Reading* magazine, Sunshine Press, Litchfield, Illinois 62056.

Sunshine Press Also Publishes
Sunshine Magazine

Besides *Good Reading* magazine, the Sunshine Press also publishes *Sunshine Magazine*, a monthly publication which is primarily human interest and inspiration in nature. Nonfiction material is needed for the following areas: My Most Extraordinary Experience: Yes, It Happened To Me; The Editor's Favorite Meditation; The Gem of the Month; The Editor's Favorite Poem; and Calling All Young People.

My Most Extraordinary Experience: Yes, It Happened To Me

- First person accounts of an unusual or spectacular true event or circumstance are wanted. The event or circumstance can be a once-in-a-lifetime occurrence (piloting the blimp or meeting the president, for example) or a situation that helped influence a life (a miraculous escape, for instance, or advice from a respected person that continues to inspire). Payment is $25.

The Editor's Favorite Meditation or **The Gem of the Month** - Material should not exceed 200 words and should be inspirational such as uplifting essays about nature and human nature. Examples are: "Thoughts for a Busy Mother," "Golden Memories," "What is an Anniversary?" or "Sunrise...Sunset." Payment is $20.

The Editor's Favorite Poem - Should not exceed 16 lines. Payment is $15.

Calling All Young People - Juvenile stories limited to 400 words and directed at ages four to fourteen. Story-type poetry, humor, true-to-life experiences and how-to articles are bought for this section. Payment varies.

Sunshine Magazine purchases First North American serial rights with the privilege of reprinting the material in any of the Sunshine Press publications. **Send the complete article or poem. Do not query.** Sample copies of **Sunshine Magazine** are available on request at $.50 each (include a SASE). Send material to *Sunshine Magazine*, Sunshine Press, Litchfield, Illinois 62056.

Following are 10 other general interest publications. Their editors are looking for freelance material. They are listed alphabetically.

THE AMERICAN LEGION

The American Legion, The Magazine for a Strong America is a recognized leader among national general interest publications and is published monthly by The American Legion for its 2.6 million members. These military service veterans, working through 16,000 community-level posts, dedicate themselves to God and country and traditional American values; a strong national security; adequate and compassionate care for veterans, their widows and orphans; community service; and the wholesome development of our nation's youth.

Freelance material is needed in the following areas: national security, foreign affairs, contemporary problems, trends of national importance, analyses of key events in American history that have lessons for today, incidents that occurred in the wars of the 20th century, sports, hobbies, health, ethics, arts and humor. Length is from 750 to 1,200 words for material written for specific departments. 1,200 to 1,500 words for general features, and up to 1,800 words for major analytical features.

Articles should adhere to a three-part editorial format: state the problem; how will it affect our readers; and what solutions are available. Before being assigned an article, writers will be required to submit an outline showing the general thrust of the proposed article.

Article payment ranges from $250 to $1,200 depending on the complexity of subject matter and on the magazine's current needs. Kill fees and reimbursement of expenses are negotiable with writers working on assignment.

The American Legion magazine usually purchases First North American serial rights. Sample copies are available for $1.50 each with SASE.

Query first. The address of *The American Legion* magazine is P. O. Box 1055, Indianapolis, Indiana 46206-1055.

THE BEST REPORT

The Best Report, "Exploring the World of Quality," is a monthly newsletter that authoritatively reports on high quality consumer goods and services, travel, collectibles, and sporting and cultural events.

Features of 750 to 1,800 words are needed. For these articles, three or more authorities should be consulted and their dissenting or concurring opinions presented with quotes. Experts' credentials should be documented; titles or positions included. Query first.

Finds of 250 to 500 words are also sought. These are short items on new and different subjects readers should know about and probably will not discover elsewhere. Finds may originate from personal experiences backed by further research. Addresses and phone numbers are usually carried at the end of each article. **Send the complete article.**

The basic payment rate is $.30 a word on publication. The address of *The Best Report* is Suite 4210, Empire State Building, 350 Fifth Avenue, New York, New York 10118.

DIALOGUE, THE MAGAZINE FOR THE VISUALLY IMPAIRED

Dialogue, The Magazine for the Visually Impaired is a quarterly publication. First-person travel experiences of visually handicapped persons, articles about participation in sports by the visually handicapped, information on new products useful to the blind, features on homemaking and recorded interviews are needed. Length varies.

Short items and fillers are wanted for these columns/departments: ABAPITA, Recipe Round-Up, Around the House, and Vox Pop. Length varies.

Pays upon acceptance, $50 maximum for articles, less for short items and fillers.

Query not required. The address is Editor, *Dialogue*, Dialogue Publications, Inc., 3100 Oak Park Avenue, Berwyn, Illinois 60402.

FORD TIMES

Ford Times is published monthly by the Ford Motor Company. The editor requests articles that primarily appeal to readers in the 18 to 35 age group. Major categories for which freelance material is needed are: topical (trends, lifestyles); profiles of interesting people, well known or otherwise, especially those with noteworthy achievements; places of interest (narrow-view pieces rather than conventional broadscope destination stories); first-person accounts of unusual vacation trips or real-life travel "adventures"; unusual sporting events or outdoor activities; humor; "Road Show" anecdotes and "Glove Compartment" items.

Full-length manuscripts of 1,200 to 1,500 words earn from $550 to $800; medium-length articles of 800 to 1,200 words earn $400; short pieces of 500 to 800 words earn $250; and "Road Show" and "Glove Compartment" items of 150 words get $50. Payment in all categories is made upon acceptance. *Ford Times* buys first-time publication rights.

Additional payment for photos ranges from $150 to $500. Transparencies (Kodachrome is the first choice) are preferred, but high quality 8" x 10" color prints and b/w glossy prints are acceptable.

Queries are required for all but anecdotes and humor pieces. Address the Editorial Department, *Ford Times*, One Illinois Center, 111 East Wacker Drive, Suite 1700, Chicago, Illinois 60601.

FRIENDLY EXCHANGE

Friendly Exchange is published quarterly by Farmers Insurance Group and is distributed to its policyholding households from Ohio to California, the western half of the United States. The magazine caters to a family audience who like such activities as travel, camping, photography, cooking, live entertainment and who care about their homes, cars and pets. *It is not an insurance publication, nor is it an employee house organ.* Freelance articles are also sought but to lesser degree on consumer topics, car care, decorating, family activities, gardening, volunteerism and personal finance. As far as style, the article should be in third-person and have anecdotes and quotes. Length should be from 1,000 to 2,000 words.

Payment for feature articles s $400 to $800 depending on length, quality of writing and research required. *Friendly Exchange* buys all rights.

Additional payment for photos. Transparencies are preferred but some b/w glossy photos are bought. Rates range from $50 to $150.

There is a 25% kill fee for articles that were assigned but not used. Free sample copies are available by submitting an addressed 9 x 12 envelope and five first-class stamps.

Query first. The address is Editor, *Friendly Exchange*, Locust at 17th, Des Moines, Iowa 50336.

PARADE

Parade is a weekly magazine. Freelance material is needed on nationally known figures, health, consumer and environmental issues, education, community activities (with national applications), the family, sports, science and science-related articles.

Articles should be current, factual, authoritative and 1,300 to 1,500 words in length. *Parade* purchases First North American Rights and will accept completed manuscripts on speculation. Assignments are made on the basis of query letters of one page. *Parade* pays a minimum of $1,000 for articles.

Additional payment for photos which can be stock photos, 8" x 10" b/w enlargements, contact sheets or transparencies; payment varies from $75 to $750.

Address the Articles Editor, *Parade*, 750 Third Avenue, New York, New York 10017.

THE SATURDAY EVENING POST

The Saturday Evening Post is published monthly and has 132 pages. Freelancers can break in by submitting an article on one of the following subjects: sports, arts, government, education, travel, religion, history, family life, animals, science, archaeology and anthropology. Length may be 500 to 4,000 words, with 2,000 the average. Photos should be submitted with the article, either 8" x 10" b/w or color prints, 35 mm or 2-1/4" x 2-1/4" color transparencies. No additional payment is made for photos.

Article payment ranges from $15 for post scripts and fillers to $1,500 for assigned articles by name writers. Buys all rights; one-time reprint and first serial rights.

Query first. The address of *The Saturday Evening Post* is 1100 Waterway Boulevard, Indianapolis, Indiana 46202.

SATURDAY REVIEW

Saturday Review is a bimonthly national magazine that deals with features on theater, music and records, dance, film, architecture and art. Each issue contains a special section reviewing the most recently published books.

Articles are sought on all aspects of contemporary life and culture, including profiles and politics as they relate to the above areas. Length should be no longer than 3,000 words.

Query or send a complete manuscript. Unpublished writers should send complete manuscripts only. With the query or complete manuscript, send published writing samples and a vita. Sample copies are available for $2.50; a magazine-size SASE should be enclosed. The address of *Saturday Review* is 214 Massachusetts Avenue, NE, Suite 460, Washington, DC 20002.

SIGNATURE

Signature, The Citicorp Diners Club Magazine, is a monthly basically for Diners Club members but subscriptions are open to all. The magazine's focus is the art of living well in the broadest sense -- travel, dining, sports, art, music, acquisitions and fitness. It is targeted toward successful business people, executives and professionals who are affluent, well-traveled and age 40.

Material from freelancers is bought for six to ten major features and eight to twelve front-of-the-book columns in each issue. Articles should be literary and journalistic in style and avoid the service-oriented "how-to" approach. Major articles run about 2,000 words in length; columns 1,300. Payment upon acceptance begins at $700.

Query and include a few recently published clips. Sample copies are available for $2.50 apiece. The address of *Signature* is 641 Lexington Avenue, New York, New York 10022.

STAR

Star is a weekly magazine. The editors are interested in good, upbeat articles, particularly aimed at women and the family. Read several issues to get a feel for the publication and type of articles needed. Length of articles varies.

Payment on publication varies, but usually falls within the $100 to $400 range for other than brief items. Query or send completed article to Editorial Administrator, *Star*, 660 White Plains Road, Tarrytown, New York 10591.

CHAPTER XII

WOMEN'S PUBLICATIONS

Women's publications address various topics such as weddings, the working woman, liberation, how to balance being a wife/mother/working woman, business, sports and fitness. There are the traditional publications such as *Ladies' Home Journal* and *McCall's*. Then there are the newer ones such as *Woman's World, Working Mother*, and *Women in Business*. Here are nine golden opportunities to sell your freelance work. The publications are listed alphabetically.

BRIDE'S

Bride's, a Conde Nast Publication - Monthly written for the first- or second-time bride in her early twenties, the groom, and their families. The purpose of the magazine is to help the young couple plan their wedding and to happily adjust to married life together.

Freelance feature articles of two lengths are needed. The shorter articles of 1,000 to 2,500 words can cover such topics as communication, in-laws, religion, careers, money, sex, children, pre-wedding jitters, housework, step-parenting, age difference and interfaith marriage. Payment is $300 to $450. The broad, generally-focused articles of 2,500 to 3,000 words can cover such topics as becoming a father, why men marry, fathers and brides and how to fight fair. Payment is $450 to $600.

Also *Bride's* publishes one book excerpt per issue, love poems in the "LOVE" column ($25 each), and reader wedding planning ideas in "Something New" ($25 each).

When preparing an article for *Bride's*, remember that it should be well-researched. For background reading, read books, magazine clippings, but do not quote secondary sources in your article. Rather, incorporate the knowledge you gain in your own words. For emphasis or explanation of important points, rely on primary research -- interviews with experts (like marriage therapists, physicians and social workers). If you have ever been married, do not overlook yourself as a source. Articles should be written in a warm, personal and upbeat style. Offer a positive solution if there is a problem stated in the article. Also keep in mind that lots of details, anecdotes, quotes and dialogue from couples and experts make an article come alive.

First-time writers for *Bride's* write on speculation. Payment for articles is made two to three weeks after acceptance. A 20% kill fee is paid if an assigned article is not published. Address your query to *Bride's* Feature Department, Conde Nast Building, 350 Madison Avenue, New York, New York 10017.

LADIES' HOME JOURNAL

Ladies' Home Journal - Monthly which stresses originality and creativity, therefore, there are no set writer's and photographer's guidelines. The best advice is to read recent issues. The editors welcome full-length feature articles of approximately 3,000 words. Query the Editor at *Ladies' Home Journal*, Three Park Avenue, New York, New York 10016.

Freelance material is also needed for "A Woman Today." Material should be approximately 1,500 words and should be written in first person and double spaced. Enclose a self-addressed, stamped envelope and mail to Box WT, *Ladies' Home Journal*.

Payment for articles varies. If you have been published before, include a few writing samples, a list of writing credits and a resume with your query. Send this material to the address below.

For back issues, send $1.50 plus $1.50 postage and handling made payable to *Ladies' Home Journal*, Back Order Department, Three Park Avenue, New York, New York 10016.

MCCALL'S

McCall's - Monthly which has a number of places and

sections a freelancer can break in. All articles will be looked at on speculation. Payment varies.

Human interest narratives - Self-help, health and fitness, psychology and humor pieces of 1,000 to 2,500 words in length. **"McCall's Salutes"** page - These are 1,000 word profiles on exceptional women. **Seasonal Stories** - *McCall's* is interested in new ways of looking at holidays. Keep in mind that Christmas comes in July at *McCall's*; send ideas well in advance. **Vital Signs** - This monthly section consists of short items of 350 to 500 words on health and medical news. *McCall's* is especially interested in recent medical breakthroughs and/or the results of studies published in professional health journals. Completed manuscripts should be accompanied by copies of all source material (for example, journal articles) and telephone numbers of those interviewed or quoted for fast-checking purposes. **VIP-ZIP** - This special section that only goes to subscribers in high-income zip code areas provides an excellent opportunity to break into the magazine. The tone is kicky and fun, with less emphasis on service than on entertainment (while still giving the reader the information he/she needs to know). Subjects covered are: travel, wine and food, finance, decorating, fashion and beauty. In all areas, *McCall's* is looking for the newest, hottest, most upscale information. The editor is especially interested in round-ups like five great-but-little-known places to stay in Ireland, or the 10 best ways to invest $10,000. Most articles run from 800 to 1,500 words.

Query the specific section editor at *McCall's*, 230 Park Avenue, New York, New York 10169.

NEW CLEVELAND WOMAN

New Cleveland Woman is a monthly publication read by over 80,000 upwardly mobile women in Cleveland and the surrounding seven-county area.

Freelance material is needed for the following departments: Picture of Success, Careers, In Business, Legally Brief, Money Matters, Healthwise, First Person Singular, Professional Style, and Exit Laughing. Money Matters, Healthwise and Legally Brief must be written by a professional in the field, or interview quotes and opinions from local experts in the field. Submission is on speculation unless an assignment was specified.

Payment is $2 per published column inch and is made on

the 15th of the month of publication.

Submit complete manuscript for Exit Laughing and First Person Singular. Query for other articles. The address is Editor, *New Cleveland Woman*, 104 E. Bridge Street, Berea, Ohio 44017.

WOMAN (R)

Woman (R) - Bimonthly looking for a variety of freelance articles. These types are needed: humor pieces, should be no more than 600 words; personal experience, should not exceed 1,500 words; Bravo Woman Column, should not exceed 1,500 words; Woman in the News, maximum of 500 words; and Let's Put Our Heads Together, maximum of 500 words. All articles are bought on speculation. Buys one-time, North American printing rights. Payment ranges from $15 to $125.

Query first. The address of *Woman* is Harris Publications Inc., 1115 Broadway, New York, New York 10010.

WOMAN'S WORLD

Woman's World, The Woman's Weekly is the only weekly woman's magazine in the United States. It offers a mix of service and feature stories and is designed to appeal to American women of all ages. Articles should be heartwarming, informative, thoroughly researched and tightly and dramatically written.

Numerous types of freelance articles are wanted for various areas. **Intro (800 to 1,000 words)** - This is an exceptionally strong story with mass appeal. Topics range from the trendy: Can You Find Love at the Health Spa?; to the controversial: Missing Children: Are the Frightening Statistics Wrong; to the universal: The Magic of Touch. These can also be human interest features. Good photos are a must. **Report** - Thoroughly-researched investigative news feature with national scope and strong interest to women. All sides of the issue must be carefully explored; all facts presented; and all major authorities must be contacted and quoted. Examples are: Can Cosmetics be Harmful to Your Health, Medical Malpractice, and Housewives Fighting Toxic Waste. **In Real Life (1,000 to 2,000 words)** - This type of article covers a dramatic moment or a crisis in someone's life. May be first person. Examples are: Six-year-old holds off attackers at gunpoint to save his mom; and After 34 years of darkness, a woman sees again. **Families (1,000 to 1,200 words)** - These articles focus on families. They give a glimpse into their lives with charming, heartwarming quotes. Examples are: They live like their grandparents; and They adopt handicapped kids. **Between You & Me (600 to 800 words)** - First person, humorous and poignant essays on slice-of-life topics. How come I do not look like women on TV and What happens when the kids start dating. **Send only complete manuscripts. Scales (1,000 to 1,200 words)** - True stories of women who have run afoul of the law -- sometimes the women committed the crime, sometimes they were the victim or the relative of a criminal. In any case, the heroine must be sympathetic and the author must get good quotes from her. An example is: She went to court to keep her son from being spanked in school and she got arrested for skinny-dipping. **Turning Point (1,200 to 1,500 words)** - Dramatic, first-person accounts of how a woman's life has changed, either through an outside influence or through a change in her own way of thinking. Writing style should be emotional and sympathetic. Examples are: I gave up my baby to give him a better life; and we had no money to buy our children gifts, but we learned the true meaning of Christmas. **Living Today (800 to 1,000 words)** - Pop-psych, self-help piece on a topic of interest to women. Style must be light, bright and very upbeat. No "psycho-talk" -- put all complicated psychological concepts in simple, easy-to-read understandable language. No "in" words like growth and actualization. The article should either be written by a psychologist with specialization in the field being covered or by a freelancer quoting one acknowledged specialist throughout. Articles should have two anecdotes describing real people (with real names and places) who have faced the problem. Your sex fantasies--are they normal?; How to raise a happy, healthy only child? and Turn your husband into your dream lover.

Payment ranges from $250 to $750. Send queries to Articles Department, *Women's World*, P. O. Box 6700, Englewood, New Jersey 07631.

WOMEN IN BUSINESS

Women in Business - Bimonthly national publication of the American Business Women's Association. Published by The ABWA Company, Inc., it has a circulation of 120,000. Readers are working women, primarily between the ages of 26 and 55; 78% are employed fulltime; 59% have college backgrounds; and 62% are married. Forty percent are managers, including company owners; 33% are office employees, including accountants, administrative assistants and secretaries; 19% are professionals, including doctors and consultants; and 8% are employed in various service positions.

Freelance articles are needed on business relations and trends, new office practices, self-improvement, issues and government regulations that affect women. All material should be carefully developed to interest working women at all levels of business. Articles should not exceed 1,500 words. Payment varies.

Query first or submit completed manuscript to *Women in Business*, 9100 Ward Parkway, P. O. Box 8728, Kansas City, Missouri 64114-0728.

WORKING MOTHER

Working Mother - Monthly that helps women in their task of juggling job, home and family. Freelance articles of 1,500 to 2,000 words are wanted. Authors should submit articles on these topics: time, home and money management, health, family relationships, single parenthood and job-related issues.

Queries should be addressed to The Editorial Department, *Working Mother*, 230 Park Avenue, New York, New York 10169.

WOMEN'S SPORTS AND FITNESS

Women's Sports and Fitness - Monthly publication devoted to women's sports, fitness and health. The average reader is between 20 and 30 and participates in two or more sports.

Freelance articles are bought for departments and feature articles are also needed. **End Zone Department** - This is a column of opinion. The piece can be political, personal, humorous or controversial, but it must be specific, well focused, substantiated and less than 1,500 words. Payment is $75. **Sports Pages Department** - This section contains short profiles of collegiate and high school athletes, as well as women of any age who show promise in the sports world, and sports-related items. Send queries to the Sports Pages Editor. **Personality Profile Features** - These are in-depth portraits of women who have achieved extraordinary results in their field, as well as of lesser-known women who would be an inspiration to readers because of their unusual accomplishments. **Off-beat and recreational sports and adventure** - These stories inform and encourage involvement in active living (examples are backpacking, aerobic dancing, windsurfing). **Non-sports authoritative articles** - The editor is looking for articles on fitness, nutrition and sports-related issues. Subjects that have been covered in the past include osteoporosis, vegetarianism, steroids and stretching exercises. Features are bought on speculation. It is best to query first. Features range from 1,500 to 3,500 words. Payment is $200 to $500 made upon publication.

Address all queries and manuscripts to the Queries Editor at *Women's Sports and Fitness*, 310 Town & Country Village, Palo Alto, California 94301. Back copies can be purchased for $2 each; one-year subscriptions are $12.

CHAPTER XIII

TRAVEL AND INFLIGHT MARKETS

If you are interested in writing for travel and inflight markets, I suggest you buy a copy of my book, *Travel Writing for Fun and Profit: How To Add Dollars To Your Income Writing Travel Articles and Getting Them Published*. The book was published in 1984 and costs $9.95, plus a charge for shipping and handling. It can be purchased from R&E Publishers, P. O. Box 2008, Saratoga, California 95070, the publisher of this book.

Definitions of travel and inflight publications follow:

1. **Travel** - These publications want only travel articles. Examples are *Travel-Holiday* and *Transitions Abroad, Guide to International Study, Work and Travel*.

2. **Inflight** - These are airline publications. Examples are *Republic*, the magazine of Republic Airlines and *United*, the magazine of United Airlines.

Travel and inflight magazine editors purchase freelance articles other than travel. These include people profiles and in-depth trend stories.

Generally, payment for freelance material in all these publications is quite high.

Subjects for travel and in-flight publications are broad. A few suggestions are:

* Museums - Milwaukee has one of the finest museums in the United States. It is called the Milwaukee Public Museum.

* Amusement Parks - Examples are Disney World, Disney-

land, Great America and Six Flags.

* Specialty Parks - These are parks that are devoted to a special interest. For example, at Kentucky Horse Park in Lexington, one can view exciting horse races as well as the horses, horse equipment and the museum.

* Gardens - Examples are Cypress and Busch Gardens.

* Mansions - In this category, I place people's lovely homes which are open to the public for viewing. Some of them are historical sites. Examples are House on the Rock near Spring Green, Wisconsin; Hearst Castle in San Simeon, California; George Washington's home in Mount Vernon, Virginia; and the Biltmore House and Gardens in Asheville, North Carolina.

* Shopping Malls - New shopping malls in your area could be a subject for a travel article.

* Wineries - I think a winery is an excellent idea for a travel article.

* Zoos - This is one place you can take your family and the cost is not that much.

* Natural Wonders - These would include mountain ranges, waterfalls, forests and deserts. Examples are the Smoky Mountains, Yellowstone National Park and Niagara Falls.

* Boat Cruises - A cruise of a specific area can make an interesting subject. For example, when I was in New York, I took a "Circle Line" cruise of Manhattan Island.

* Raft Trips - This is another possibility. When I was out west a few years ago, I took the mild raft trip down the Snake River in Jackson, Wyoming. This is one trip that you really enjoy and you do not get that wet.

* Historic Sites - These are favorites such as the United Nations, the White House, Statue of Liberty and Jefferson Memorial.

* An Individual City or Country - This is the usual subject for a travel article. For example, what is exciting and interesting about Philadelphia, Denver, Milwaukee, or what makes France, London or Italy unique?

Example of My Published Travel Article

Since writing travel articles is one of my specialties, I would like to present one of my articles (about 800 words on Philadelphia) which appeared in the **Grand Rapids Press** newspaper on November 4, 1984. It appeared on the Sunday travel page. The title of the article is "History Comes Alive

In This City" and it had one b/w glossy photo of Independence Hall. The verbatim text is as follows:

By Ruth Wucherer

PHILADELPHIA - United States history is brought vividly to life in Philadelphia's Independence National Historical Park.

Take your best waking shoes because there is much to see. Allow at least three or more days to see all the sites.

The main area of Independence National Historical Park extends from 2nd to 6th Streets between Walnut and Chestnut Streets.

The National Park Service, U. S. Department of the Interior, is responsible for maintaining the buildings which were constructed in the 1700s and early 1800s. Some of the buildings are: Independence Hall, Congress Hall, Carpenters' Hall, Liberty Bell Pavilion and the Graff House.

Begin touring the area by first stopping at the Visitor Center on 3rd and Chestnut Streets. Here you can view a 28-minute film titled "Independence."

Also obtain your free admission tickets for touring Independence Hall at the Visitor Center.

Your next stop is Carpenter's Hall. Here the First Continental Congress met from Sept. 5 to Oct. 26, 1774. In this hall, the Congress and its leader, Samuel Adams, defined colonial rights and denied the power of Parliament to limit them.

They also gave a voice to Colonial grievances and pledged the colonies not to trade with Britain until these grievances were redressed. Visitors can actually see the chairs on which Congress members sat.

The building of Carpenters' Hall started in 1763 by the company of the same name. Carpenters' Company is patterned after the guilds of England and is today the oldest builder's organization in the United States. At present, this company operates Carpenters' Hall.

Two of the focal points of the park are Independence Hall and Square.

You must have a ticket from the Visitor Center to take a tour of Independence Hall. Independence Hall, a brick structure, was built between 1732 and 1756 and restored in 1970.

Tour guides enthusiastically tell tourists what happened in the hall's various rooms. In the first floor Assembly Room, the Second Continental Congress adopted the Declaration of Independence in July of 1776.

In 1787 the Federal Convention, under the leadership of George Washington, framed the Constitution of the United States.

Across the hallway is the Supreme Court Chamber of Pennsylvania, where judges declared freedom and sentenced lawbreakers. Outside the hall is Independence Square, where the Declaration of Independence was first read in public on July 8, 1776.

Near Independence Hall is Congress Hall, which was the meeting place for the U. S. Congress from 1790 to 1800. On the first floor is the chamber of the House of Representatives, where John Adams took the presidential oath. On the second floor is the U. S. Senate Chamber and committee rooms.

Across the street from Independence Hall is the Liberty Bell Pavilion. The 2,080 pound bell pealed loudly on July 8, 1776 to proclaim the first reading of the Declaration of Independence.

But 80 years later, when it cracked, it was removed from active service. The bell was originally ordered for the Pennsylvania State House (Independence Hall) to commemorate founder William Penn's Charter of Privileges.

It has twice been recast. Today the Liberty Bell is enclosed in a glass pavilion which serves as its permanent home. The bell was moved on December 31, 1975 from Independence Hall to this pavilion.

From the inside, visitors can touch and take pictures of the bell and hear tapes in English and six other languages giving its history.

Close to the Liberty Bell Pavilion is the Graff House, which is a reconstruction of the house in which Thomas Jefferson drafted the Declaration of Independence in June of 1776.

He was said to have done the drafting in the second floor parlor of this house built by bricklayer Jacob Graff, Jr. An audiovisual presentation gives visitors the important details about the drafting. The Graff House was originally built in 1775 and reconstructed in 1975.

Besides the Independence National Historical Park complex, I feel the visitors should see these three additional sites. They are Franklin Court, Christ Church and the Betsy Ross

House.

Franklin Court is named after Benjamin Franklin, who played such important roles in American history.

Located on Market Street between 3rd and 4th Streets, the Court is the site of five rowhouses once owned by Franklin, including the remains of one in which he lived from 1763 to 1812. The court was built from 1763 to 1787, and restored and reconstructed in 1976.

Beneath the courtyard is the B. Free Franklin Post Office and Museum. The museum on the second floor has displays of rare postage stamps, unusual philatelic products and postal artifacts from the Revolutionary War period to the present.

The Pony Express saddle mail pouch, the first mailboxes used to receive mail, and the first type of cancellation equipment used by the post offices are among the exhibits.

Christ Church, on 2nd between Market and Arch Streets, was the house of worship of fifteen signers of the Declaration of Independence, two of whom are buried in the churchyard. Founded in 1695, the church typifies early Georgian architecture.

Lastly, the Betsy Ross House, 239 Arch Street, is where the famed colonial seamstress supposedly stitched the first American flag in 1776. The restored home is furnished in the middle-class manner of the period.

What makes Independence National Historical Park and the surrounding sites even more appealing is that there are no admission charges, except at the Deshler-Morris House in Germantown. George Washington occupied this home during brief periods in 1793 and 1794.

There are streets around the park where you can park your car, although I recommend walking from the heart of Philadelphia to this area. It is not that far.

The streets are very narrow and one way and, unless you are used to them, are somewhat difficult to drive on.

As far as staying at a hotel in Philadelphia, I recommend staying at one away from Independence National Historical Park because hotels are very expensive in this area.

I stayed at the Holiday Inn--Center City on 18th and Market Streets which is moderately priced. The hotel is waking distance from the park.

The Philadelphia Convention and Visitors Bureau offers a number of free materials to help you plan your trip.

(Editor's note: Ruth Wucherer is a free-lance writer from

Milwaukee.)

I would like to point out these things about the article:
1. In the newspapers, editors put a dateline in capital letters at the beginning of the article (in this case, PHILADELPHIA). It appears that I wrote the article in Philadelphia but I actually wrote it after I returned home.
2. The paragraphs are short which is characteristic of newspaper style. Magazine articles have longer sentences.
3. My article was hardly altered at all.
4. I like the way certain paragraphs are highlighted in bold face. The editor did this. It is an effective technique to capture the attention of the reader.
5. I like the title of the article, "History Comes Alive In This City." It sets the tone of the article for Philadelphia is very historical city.
6. The sixth paragraph tells the reader about free admission tickets for touring Independence Hall at the visitor center. Always include things that are free in a travel article.
7. The third to last paragraph says that the Holiday Inn--Center City on 18th and Market Streets, where I stayed, is moderately priced. This is helpful information for the reader. I think I had the price range but the editor did not include it in the final published article.
8. The last paragraph on the Philadelphia Visitors Convention and Visitors Bureau is also useful to the reader for this bureau provides a number of free materials for a traveler to plan his/her trip. I think I had the address of the bureau but the editor did not include it.
9. The article not only covers Independence National Historical Park but also surrounding sites such as Franklin Court, Christ Church, and the Betsy Ross House. What makes visiting these places so special is that there are no admission charges.
10. I like that the editor gave me a byline at the beginning of the article and the editor's note at the end of the article. I have written several travel articles for the ***Grand Rapids Press*** newspaper. This is probably why I received a byline.

Travel Markets

I recommend that you send travel articles to the following

two travel magazines.

TRAVEL-HOLIDAY

Travel-Holiday - Monthly which purchases three types of articles: features, featurettes, and here and there. Buys first North American rights. Pays upon acceptance.

Features - Articles of 1,600 to 1,800 words should deal with foreign or domestic travel destinations, off-the-beaten-path or well-known but with a new twist or update. Copy must be lively, entertaining, informative and serviceable and should include information on both daytime and evening activities if applicable. The readers should feel as if they are actually there. They must also be able to duplicate the trip, but, more importantly, they must want to. Text should be written in the author's most comfortable style. Use of anecdotes is okay in moderation. Honest, critical evaluations are most important: no guidebook rehashing. A resource box containing hard facts (where to write for further information and how to get there) must accompany all articles. Sidebars (a mini-article relating to the article) of no more than 500 words are acceptable. Payment is $400. Features should be accompanied by a varied selection of transparencies or sources where they can be obtained. On the whole, photography is assigned to a professional photographer.

Featurettes - Small towns or cities as well as museums, markets, shopping sites, art galleries and similar subjects of special interest will be considered as featurettes (800 to 1,300 words).

Special aspects of a major destination -- Savannah's Historical Inns, Milwaukee's Ethnic Festivals -- are also suitable for submission. Payment is $250 and up.

Here & There - Any unique topic that can be covered succinctly with one piece of black and white art, that is travel-related and deserves special recognition (i.e., the film studio where "Das Boot" was made, the Football Halls of Fame, the Texas Chili Cook-Off) and can be covered in *575 words* will be considered for Here & There. Pieces must be *written very tightly*, and must really jump out and grab the reader. When querying for this section, please send suggested lead and indicate "Here & There" in your cover letter. Payment is $150. Sample copies for writers are available for $1.00. Enclose a check or money order when requesting a sample copy. Query the Editor at *Travel-Holiday*, Travel

Building, Floral Park, New York, New York 11001.

TRANSITIONS ABROAD, GUIDE TO INTERNATIONAL STUDY, WORK AND TRAVEL

Transitions Abroad, Guide to International Study, Work, and Travel - A bimonthly magazine for active international travelers of all ages. Readers are seeking information and firsthand reports on living, working, and learning in another culture. They want more than a tourist's view of the world. Freelance feature articles of up to 1,500 words are needed that describe how "total immersion" is possible, even (or especially) on a small budget.

Material is also wanted for these departments in every issue: Traveler's Advisory/Resources, Information Exchange, Adult Study/Travel, Inside Travel, Back Door Travel, Abroad in Books (reviews), Adventure Travel, Foreign Study Roundtable, Foreign Study/Travel Program Information and Participants' Reports.

Payment is $1.00-$1.50 per column inch. Rights revert to the writer. A sample copy is $3.50 which includes postage and handling. Query the editor at *Transitions Abroad*, Box 344, Amherst, Massachusetts 01004.

INFLIGHT PUBLICATIONS

Submit your article ideas to these ten inflight publications and you are bound to make a sale!

CONTINENTAL MAGAZINE

Continental Magazine is the monthly inflight publication of Continental Airlines. Types of articles needed are: lifestyle, leisure, celebrity and success profiles, pieces on successful business endeavors and entrepreneurs, business in general, health and medicine, high tech, finance, food, wine, exercise, recreation and restaurants. Length varies. All articles should include quotes, anecdotes and documentation of facts.

Pays upon publication: $250 to $400 for column or department material of 1,000 to 2,000 words and $500 to $700 for full-length features of 2,500 words or more.

Query first. The address is Editor, *Continental Magazine*, Brighton Square Publications, 901 Mopac Expressway South, Suite 350, Barton Oaks Plaza One, Austin, Texas 78746.

EAST/WEST NETWORK PUBLICATIONS
The East/West Network, Inc. publishes a number of inflight publications. In general:
* Each magazine comes out monthly.
* Each contains a destination travel feature.
* Query with published works.
* All buy first rights only.
* Length ranges from 1,000 to 2,500 words.
* Payment varies.
* Sample copies are $2.00 each.

The Los Angeles office publishes the following magazines: *Ozark, PSA Magazine, Republic, Spirit and Western's World*. If you have an article idea, query the Editor, at the specific publication. The address of the Los Angeles office is 5900 Wilshire Boulevard, Los Angeles, California 90036. Descriptions of the magazines follow. They are listed alphabetically.

OZARK
Ozark, The Magazine of the Midwest - Has a Midwestern focus. It accents the good life and healthy business climate in the Midwest. The editor wants features on business, personalities, fashion, sports, arts, and food. This is the inflight magazines of Ozark Airlines.

PSA MAGAZINE
PSA Magazine - Needs feature articles for personalities/question and answer, environment/conservation, sports, arts and business. Also needs material for calendar listings; business trends; and regular columns -- restaurants, saloons, show business, finance, sports, and health. Covers California, Nevada, Arizona, Washington, Oregon and Idaho. This is the inflight magazine of Pacific Southwest Airlines.

REPUBLIC
Republic - Coverage is national. Editorial emphasis is on contemporary popular culture, business and sports. The publication is for the Midwestern executive who savors success at home, at work and at play. Needs articles for its regular departments including Technology, Sports, Media, Business, On The Go (travel trends), Americana, Health, Personal Style, Innovators, Dining Out, and On Wheels. Inflight magazine of Republic Airlines.

SPIRIT
Spirit - Primarily Texas and Southwest coverage. Edited for Southwest's sophisticated passengers, the magazine employs superior writing and graphics to explore the business, arts and lifestyles of the most progressive region in America.

WESTERN'S WORLD
Western's World - The magazine has features that present the panorama of people and enterprises that are "winning the West." *Western's World* departments guide readers in discovering outdoor adventures, fine dining, superb accommodations, trends and technology. To sum up, the magazine mixes business and pleasure in a fashion designed to appeal to the mover and shaker and the vacationer. Coverage primarily west of the Rockies, plus New York, Alaska, Hawaii and Mexico. Inflight magazine of Western Airlines.

The New York office of East/West Network, Inc. publishes the following publications: *Clipper, Northwest Orient* and *United*. These inflight magazines are arranged alphabetically. If you have an article idea, query the Editor at the specific publication. The address is: (Name of Publication), East/West Network, Inc., 34 East 51st Street, New York, New York 10022.

CLIPPER
Clipper - This publication is designed and edited to appeal to the sophisticated business and pleasure traveler on Pan Am's domestic and international routes. Articles are urbane in tone with an affluent audience in mind. The editor wants articles on travel, the arts, science and technology, business, sports, food and beverages fashion, adventure and humor. Coverage is worldwide. Inflight magazine of Pan Am Airlines.

NORTHWEST ORIENT
Northwest Orient - The magazine is a mix of features that contain the underlying theme of influence...people who influence the arts, the sciences; products that influence cultures across the Atlantic, across the Pacific. Special emphasis is placed on the Orient, since it is the most important American-based carrier to Japan, Hong Kong, Korea and the Philippines. Emphasis is also given to Northern Europe. This is the inflight magazine of Northwest Orient Airlines.

UNITED

United - Needs travel articles for the business person and for offbeat vacationing. The editor wants features on executive lifestyles and business related matters. Material is also needed for art portfolios; high-level new products of interest to executives; and for regular columns -- travel, sports, driving and personal finance. Coverage includes major U. S. cities, Japan and Hong Kong. Inflight magazine of United Airlines.

USAIR

USAir - Monthly magazine needs travel articles which focus on the U.S. The editors are looking for articles on general interest subjects including business, sports, nature, the arts, science technology, food, Americana, education, health, personal finance humor, and any others that are appropriate for a wide audience. Articles should be crisply written, lively, and positive in approach. USAir is a domestic carrier. Therefore, do not send articles on Toronto and Montreal.

The editors are especially seeking articles that can be illustrated with striking photographs or artwork. The writer does not have to supply the photos. This is mostly done by professional photographers. Articles should range in length between 1,500 and 4,000 words, for which *USAir* pays $400 to $1,000. *USAir* buys first rights and pays upon acceptance.

Query first. Queries should be brief, but explain what the article is about, its relevance to a wide audience in the 1980s, the main points you want to cover, and the length you have in mind. Clips of previously published articles will help convince the editors that you can write.

A sample copy is $3.00. Write the Editor at *USAir*, 600 Third Avenue, New York, New York 10016.

CHAPTER XIV

AUTO AND/OR TRAVEL CLUB PUBLICATIONS

Another type of publication you can submit your article to is an auto and/or travel club magazine. These publications are distributed to members of an auto and/or travel club. Besides travel articles, the editors of these publications purchase people profiles and indepth trend stories. Payment to authors is usually quite high. The following four publications are looking for your articles. They are listed alphabetically.

CHEVRON USA
Chevron USA - Quarterly magazine published for the Chevron Travel Club. Areas covered by the magazine include the United States, Canada, Baja California, Puerto Rico, the Virgin Islands, Guam, and American Samoa.

Articles of 700 words are particularly needed for the Family Activities section. The subjects for this type of article are craft how-to's, indoor and outdoor games, and other activities families can pursue together. Sometimes they are seasonal in nature. Features of 700 o 1,600 words are needed. Topics can include attractions in or near metropolitan areas, such as historical sites, recreation areas, museums, and other places of interest. Pictorials, theme articles, and features about sports, games, the outdoors and wildlife are also needed. *Chevron* also wants original travel anecdotes of a maximum length of 200 words. Send the complete manuscript.

Payment for features is $150 to $500, or approximately $.30 per word. Payment is made upon acceptance. Payment for travel anecdotes is $25 and is made upon publication.

Queries from established writers are welcomed but completed manuscripts are preferred from unpublished writers. For first-time contributors to *Chevron USA*, a few tearsheets of your best published material (travel-related) are helpful. Unless a specific assignment is made, editors consider all material on a speculation basis only.

Any questions, write the Editor at *Chevron USA Odyssey*, 2001 The Alameda, P. O Box 6227, San Jose, California 95150.

FORD TIMES

Ford Times - Monthly published by the Ford Motor Company. Although it is published by an auto company, *Ford Times* prints no more automotive-related articles than do most general-interest publications targeted for a family audience. The primary editorial goal is to be lively, informative, contemporary, and, above all, interesting.

Articles should appeal to readers in the 18 to 35 years age group. Articles wanted are: topical (trends, lifestyles); places of interest (narrow-view pieces rather than conventional broad-scope destination stores; e.g., the guest house of New Orleans' French Quarter rather than New Orleans in general); profiles of interesting people, well-known or otherwise; first-person accounts of unusual vacation trips or real-life travel "adventures," unusual sporting events or outdoor activities; and humor (ranging from vacation/travel/dining anecdotes for "Road Show" to full-length articles or essays).

Payment is made upon acceptance and depends on the length of the article. Full-length articles ranging from 1,200 to 1,500 words earn $550 to $800; medium-length from 800 to 1,200 words, $400; and short length from 500 to 800 words, $250. One-third kill fees are paid on assigned articles that are rejected. "Road Show" anecdotes and "Glove Compartment" items (up to 150 words) earn $50. Payment is made upon acceptance. *Ford Times* buys first-time publication rights.

Queries are required for all but anecdotes and humor pieces. Query the editors at *Ford Times*, One Illinois Center, 111 East Wacker Drive, Suite 1700, Chicago, Illinois 60601.

VISTA/USA

Vista/USA, The Magazine of Exxon Travel Club - Quarterly magazine which is distributed to about 850,000 club members throughout the U. S. Wants feature articles of 1,800 to 2,500 words on the U. S., Canada, Mexico and the Caribbean. Articles should generally relate to travel but should avoid hard-core travel information such as where to stay, where to dine, prices and hours. Emphasis should be on the flavor of an area, using a thematic approach that brings out what is unusual about it from the writer's point of view. The writer should use anecdotes and quotes. In addition to feature articles, special articles are needed. These are hobby/collecting pieces, general culture articles, Americana, personality profiles with a travel tie-in and articles on vacations for seniors (but not how-tos).

Payment for feature and special articles starts at $600. Queries are preferred for features, in narrative, outline form. The approach, as well as the subject matter, should be defined. Include samples of your published clips with the query.

Shorter articles are needed for the following departments: American Vignettes, Close Focus, and Mini Trips. **American Vignettes** (500 to 1,000 words, minimum payment of $150) covers anything travel related that also reveals a slice of American life, often with a light or humorous touch, such as asking directions from a cranky New Englander, or covering the phenomenon of "talking" license plates. **Close Focus** (800 to 1,000 words, minimum payment of $250) covers new or changing aspects of major attractions or small and limited attractions not appropriate for a feature article. **Mini-Trips** (800 to 1,000 words, minimum payment of $250) are point-to-point or loop driving tours of from 50 to 350 miles covering a variety of attractions and activities along the way. For shorter articles, the writer should submit the complete manuscript or query.

For further information, write the Editor at *Vista/USA*, General Drafting Co., Inc., Convent Station, New Jersey 07961.

THE WESTWAYS WRITER

The Westways Writer is published monthly by the Automobile Club of Southern California. Buys articles on Southern California and Western states, Mexico, Hawaii and, world travel. All articles are bought on speculation. Length is 1,500 word maximum except for Wit & Wisdom (750 to 1,000 words) and Around the Southland (1,000 words). Payment varies and is made 30 days prior to scheduled publication month.

Photos should be included with articles: 35 mm color slides or color transparencies are needed; $50 payment per photo, higher for cover. Payment is made upon publication.

Buys first rights. Query the Editor at *The Westways Writer*, P. O. Box 2890, Terminal Annex, Los Angeles, California 90051.

CHAPTER XV

REGIONAL MARKETS

Closely allied to travel, inflight, auto and/or travel club publications are regional markets. The editors of these publications are looking for many types of articles. They are searching for articles on travel, business, entertainment and the arts. These publications cover a city, state or region.

The following pages contain 23 golden opportunities for you to sell your regional articles. They are listed alphabetically.

AAA MICHIGAN LIVING

AAA Michigan Living - A monthly which informs more than one million Auto Club of Michigan members about tourist and recreational opportunities in Michigan, the U. S. and Canada. Articles should have a Michigan slant since all readers are state residents and will be traveling from a Michigan base. Recreational pursuits such as special events, camping, winter sports and outdoor activities should be stressed.

According to the "Guide for Freelance Material," *AAA Michigan Living* readers want articles that verbally and colorfully transport them to the area described, yet avoid travel writing cliches such as "Paradise for sightseers" or "Mecca for camera fans." Travel attractions should be appraised honestly and objectively, giving both good and bad points. In addition to describing things to see and do, articles should contain accurate, current information on costs the traveler would incur. On the strength of the article alone, readers should be able to decide whether or not they would enjoy visiting the area by the sounds, sights, tastes and smells described.

The editors rarely buy articles without photos. Writers can obtain photos from various tourist offices free of charge. Photos and color slides from tourist offices should be acknowledged. Black and white photography submitted is considered part of the article payment. Payment for articles, 500 to 800 words, ranges between $150 to $300. Payment is made upon acceptance. Additional payment is made for color slides or transparencies (*AAA Michigan Living* cannot accept color prints). Color photo payment is $350 for a cover photo and $50 to $75 per inside color shot depending on quality, quantity and size used. Color photography purchased will not be returned unless a special request is made for one-time only rights.

AAA Michigan Living welcomes queries from freelancers but commitments are not made on that basis. Before a decision is made to buy, the editor must see a completed article. Address articles to: Manuscripts--Publications, *AAA Michigan Living*, 17000 Executive Plaza Drive, Dearborn, Michigan 48126.

ALASKA

Alaska, The Magazine of Life on the Last Frontier-Circulation is about 170,000; nearly 75% of *Alaska's* readers live outside of Alaska. ***Monthly magazine which relies heavily on freelance contributions.*** First-person articles are needed on these subjects: hunting, fishing, mining, art/artist, historical, adventure, natural resources research, individual profile, hiking, bicycling, canoeing, kayaking, climbing, skiing (usually cross-country), dog mushing, lifestyle and cultural -- almost no subject is out of bounds, especially if it has a uniquely Alaska slant. Most of the articles range in length from 1,000 to 2,500 words, but sometimes could run up to 6,000 words which would be spread over two issues. Fillers of about 200 words are bought for the "From Ketchikan to Barrow" column. They should have a color or black-and-white photo. Fillers of 50 to 500 words are bought for the regional supplement. The material submitted should be news, business news especially, with little to interest people living outside Alaska.

Articles with photos have a better chance of being accepted. They should be original color transparencies (slides) or 8" x 10" b/w glossy prints. Historical b/w prints, for which negatives are not available, can be submitted in any size. Photos should be sharp and properly exposed. Package submissions carefully, include fact-filled captions and send by certified mail/return receipt.

Payment is up to $400 for an article-photo package (longer, feature length material). A writer will be paid $250 to $325 for an average length feature. For fillers, payment varies depending on the editor's interest in the subject and the work necessary for the writer to obtain the material. *Alaska* usually purchases one-time rights to articles and photos. Query the Editors at *Alaska*, P. O. Box 99050, Anchorage, Alaska 99509-9050.

BALTIMORE MAGAZINE

Baltimore Magazine - A monthly focusing exclusively on people, places, and things in the Baltimore metropolitan area. Current circulation is more than 50,000. Readers of *Baltimore Magazine* have a medium family income of roughly $45,000 a year, their average age is 40, and most have completed college and own their homes.

About 50% of the material in the magazine is freelance written. Articles run from 500 to several thousand words. They generally fall into these categories: consumer advice, description of local products and services; news and investigative news; profile and interview; life-style; issue discussion and explanation; descriptive and narrative; personal experience or autobiography advocacy; news analysis; arts criticism; and humor.

Payment ranges from $20 for a very short piece to several hundred dollars for a long feature. The amount of payment depends on the length of the piece, the importance of the subject, the effort required of the writer, and the quality of the manuscript. Pays upon publication. Write the circulation department for a sample copy which costs $2.34. Address query to the Managing Editor, *Baltimore Magazine*, 26 S. Calvert Street, Baltimore, Maryland 21202.

CONNECTICUT MAGAZINE

Connecticut Magazine is a general interest, service and issue-oriented monthly magazine which covers all aspects of life in the state. Readers are generally affluent and well-educated.

Freelance articles assigned on speculation are accepted on the following subjects: service, in-depth investigative, sports, business and the arts. Freelancers should query in a letter which contains a detailed outline of the proposed piece and a list of sources for the article. Length requirements range from 1,800 to 3,000 words. Payment is made upon publication. Query the Managing Editor, *Connecticut Magazine*, 636 Kings Highway, Fairfield, Connecticut 06430.

GREATER PORTLAND

Greater Portland - Quarterly magazine with a circulation of about 10,000. It is published by the Chamber of Commerce of the Greater Portland region. Freelance features of 1,000 to 2,500 words are needed for the following areas: personal profiles, place profiles, trend pieces, historical pieces, and personal essays. Personal profiles should cover interesting Great Portlanders. Place profiles should be about Greater Portland locales. Trend pieces should be about significant developments, well-known or unknown, in the life of the city. Subjects may be historical, contemporary, or projected developments of a social, cultural, artistic, intellectual, or commercial nature. Trend pieces are not news stories, but the thoughtful, informed reflections of a perceptive observer of Greater Portland life. Historical pieces deal with the region's people, places, events, and ways of life. Such pieces must have a tie to the present. Personal essays reflect on some aspect of life in and around Portland.

According to the Writer's Guidelines, "mere description or narration won't do; nor will superficial treatment of a broad or hazily defined subject. Bring one very specific aspect of Portland's life to light in such a way that your subject says something about the city as a whole. Include diverse perspectives on your subject when appropriate."

Payment ranges from $100 to $250 upon publication. New writers should submit clips of their published articles with their queries.

Query the Editor at *Greater Portland*, 142 Free Street, Portland, Maine 04101.

INDIANAPOLIS

Indianapolis - Monthly which uses in-depth articles on analysis of local issues, features on local people, organizations, and problems. They must have a strong Indianapolis or Central Indiana connection. "Indianapolis" includes Marion and the seven surrounding counties. There are regular departmental sections on business, money, leisure, sports, politics, arts, health, lifestyle and consumer information. Payment ranges from $40 to $325 depending upon research, content, experience, style and subject. Pays upon publication.

Use the Associated Press Stylebook for punctuation, grammar and preferred spellings. Use Webster's New World Dictionary, Second College Edition for spellings.

Query the Editor at *Indianapolis*, Thirty-Two East Washington Street, Indianapolis, Indiana 46204. A sample copy costs $2.10.

INDIANAPOLIS MONTHLY

Indianapolis Monthly - Covers central Indiana. Has a circulation of 40,000. Freelance articles are needed for the following areas: expose (in depth reporting on government, education, health, if it is fairly presented); general interest (sport, business, media, health); historical/nostalgic (pertaining to Indiana landmarks only; no first-person); design (at-home features about a unique home, 1,000 words maximum, transparencies or slides with cutlines); interview/profile (of regional personalities, success stories about Indiana natives); photo features (seasonal material from Indiana); travel (weekends in Indiana, no first-person). Always looking for fresh angles on Indianapolis 500. No first-person narratives, domestic humor or poetry. Query with clips of published work or send completed manuscript. Length 500 to 3,000 words. Usually buys first rights.

Photos are especially welcomed with articles. B/w glossies with good contrast. $25 per published b/w, $35 per published color transparency. Buys one-time right. Submit at least 12 transparencies on one subject for photo essay. Cutlines or I.D. lines a must. Prefer 2-1/4" transparencies or 35 mm slides.

Sample copy if $1.75. The address is: Editor, *Indianapolis Monthly*, 8425 Keystone Crossing, Suite 225, Indianapolis, Indiana 46240.

THE IOWAN

The Iowan is a quarterly magazine and the showcase publication for the state. It is a general interest magazine dedicated to presenting, through stunning color and exciting features, all that is outstanding about Iowa. *The Iowan* is a full-color publication with a 9x12 inch page format.

Most of the features are handled on an assignment basis but unsolicited manuscripts and photographs are reviewed. All articles must have color transparencies or black and white photos either taken by the author or by one of *The Iowan's* regular photographers. Read several issues of the magazine and come up with a query.

Payment is made upon publication and depends on the length of the feature. It is usually negotiated on an individual basis. For example, a feature of 1,000 words would bring approximately $125 to $175. Additional payment is made for photos.

Any questions, write the Editor at *The Iowan*, Editorial and Advertising Office, 214 Ninth Street, Des Moines, Iowa 50309.

KANSAS

Kansas is a four-color magazine published by the Kansas Department of Economic Development to promote the beauty and economy of the state. It is published quarterly in March, June, September and December and every attempt is made to feature seasonal material in each issue. It now has 40,000 paid subscribers.

Articles on each of the five regions of the state are included in each issue. They cover the arts, history, education, business and industry of Kansas. Articles must have the potential for good photography. Photos are the highlight of the magazine and the editor is only interested in articles with good photo possibilities.

Article length should be about 5 to 7 pages of double-spaced, typewritten material. The writer's full address and social security number should be on the first page of the article.

Payment for articles ranges between $75 to $150. The writer may also submit photographs or the photography may be separately assigned. Payment for photos is $25 for each scenic photograph, $35 for an inside or back cover photo, and $50 to $75 for a cover photo. *Kansas* pays roughly $100 plus mileage and expenses to photographers on assignment.

Kansas purchases first rights to both articles and photographs. The editor prefers working with Kansas writers and photographers but accepts material from out-of-state writers. Query the Editor at *Kansas*, Kansas Department of Economic Development, 503 Kansas Avenue, 6th Floor, Topeka, Kansas 66603.

MID-ATLANTIC COUNTRY

Mid-Atlantic Country - Monthly magazine for which material should be focused on some part (or all of) the Mid-Atlantic region -- Virginia, Maryland, West Virginia, Delaware, Southern Pennsylvania, North Carolina, Southern New Jersey, and Washington, D.C. The article should have a local or regional angle.

Articles can cover a range of subjects from outdoor sports to history, from arts and crafts to real estate, from human interest stories to travel/destination articles, from food to interior design.

All material is submitted on a "speculation only" basis. Pays upon publication, $3.50 per column inch, or $.10 per published word. Query the Editor at *Mid-Atlantic Monthly*, The Atrium, Suite 205, 277 South Washington Street, Alexandria, Virginia 22314.

MONTANA MAGAZINE

Montana Magazine is published in January, March, May, July, September and November. The editors are interested in entertaining and informative material on the Montana lifestyle, issues, history, community profiles, personality profiles, economy, wildlife, recreation, where to and how to enjoy and preserve the Montana landscape. Writers should submit one or two sentence author biography that shows their competence with or interest in the subject. Writers should provide photos with their articles.

Rates of payment are: feature-length articles from 1,000 to 3,000 words and their supporting photos, $75 to $150; short pieces from 400 to 1,000 words, $50 to $75; color photos, $40 to $50; color cover photo, $75; and b/w glossy photos separate from article, $10. Payment is made within 30 days of publication. Most material is purchased on a one-time rights basis which does not require the written exchange of copyright from freelancer to Montana Magazine.

Query the Editor, *Montana Magazine*, P. O. Box 5630, Helena, Montana 59604.

NEVADA

Nevada, The Magazine of the Real West is published bimonthly by the State of Nevada. The magazine is geared toward promoting tourism in Nevada.

Articles and photos are accepted on speculation and must be about Nevada, its people, history, recreation, entertainment, or scenery. Length varies. Color photos should be 35 mm, 4" x 5" or 2-1/4" transparencies. B/w photos should be 5" x 7" or 8" x 10" glossies.

Payment ranges from $50 to $300 for words and $10 to $75 for photos. Buys first North American rights.

Query first. The address is Editor, *Nevada*, Capitol Complex, Carson City, Nevada 89710.

NEW HAMPSHIRE PROFILES

New Hampshire Profiles is a statewide, glossy, four-color magazine about New Hampshire. Its intent is to profile what is exciting, unique and special in the state.

Feature article material is needed as well as material for these departments: Calendar of Events, Looking Back, Shelf Life, The Last Word, Dateline Granite State, Our Town, Food, Nature Watch, Arts, Dream House, People, and New Hampshire Roadways. Length varies.

Pays upon publication. Buys first rights. Article payment: full-length features, $300; short features and involved columns, $150 to $200; and very short pieces, $75.

Query first. The address of *New Hampshire Profiles* is 90 Fleet Street, P. O. Box 4638, Portsmouth, New Hampshire 03801.

NEW YORK MAGAZINE

New York Magazine - Needs weekly articles relating to New York City. Preferred topics include profiles of New Yorkers, health/medicine, behavior/lifestyle, investigative reporting, and service articles (articles giving consumers guidance on matters ranging from where to shop to how to determine which bank will give you the best service). Features are also accepted on the arts, politics, business, fashion, the media, and advertising. However, there is a regular stable of staff columnists who cover these topics.

Word length varies from 1,800 to 5,000 words and payment varies. Query first with as much detail as possible. Samples of previously published work should be included. Write the

Editor, *New York Magazine*, 755 Second Avenue, New York, New York 10017.

NORTH COAST VIEW

North Coast View - Monthly magazine covering entertainment, recreation, the arts, consumer news, and in-depth news for Humboldt County audience consisting mostly of 18 to 50 year olds. Circulation is 20,000.

Freelance articles are needed for the following areas: Book excerpts (locally written); expose (consumer, government); historical/nostalgic (local); humor; interview/profile (entertainment, recreation, arts or political people planning to visit Humboldt County); new product (for arts); photo feature (locals for art section); and travel (weekend and short retreats accessible from Humboldt County). "Most features need a Humboldt County slant." Special issues include Kinetic Sculpture Race (May), Christmas (Dec.), and St. Patrick's Day (March). Buys 30 to 40 manuscripts/year. Query with published clips or send completed manuscript. Length should be 1,250 to 2,500 words. Pays $25 to $75.

Articles are also needed for columns/departments: Outdoors (outdoor activities in Humboldt County including crabbing, fishing, boating, skiing); A La Carte (restaurant reviews of county restaurants); Ex Libris (books); Reel Views (film); Vinyl Views (albums); Cornucopia (calendar); Poetry; Rearview (art). Buys 80 to 100 manuscripts/year. Send completed manuscript. Length should be 500 to 750 words. Pays $10 to $25.

Generally buys all rights, but will reassign. Payment varies and is upon publication. Sample copy $1; free writer's guidelines. For further information, write the Publishers/Editors at *North Coast View*, Blarney Publishing, Box 1374, Eureka, California 95502.

NORTHEAST OUTDOORS

Northeast Outdoors is a monthly publication which deals with camping and outdoor activities in the Northeastern States -- New England, New York, New Jersey and Pennsylvania.

Articles are needed on good campgrounds and destinations, travel throughout the region, how-to pieces about camping and recreational vehicles, and pieces on camp-related outdoor activities. The first person approach is preferred. Articles can range in length from 2 to 10 pages, but 5 to 8 pages is the norm.

B/w glossy photos (3" x 5" to 8" x 10") should be submitted with the article). Additional payment for photos. Pays upon publication; $30 to 40 for articles without photos and up to $80 for articles with photos.

Queries are not required. Send completed manuscript and photos to the Editor at *Northeast Outdoors*, 70 Edwin Avenue, P. O. Box 2180, Waterbury, Connecticut 06722.

OHIO

Ohio - Monthly magazine. Freelance articles are needed for six areas: features, columns, Ohioana, Ohioans, Ohioguide, and Diner's Digest. **Features** vary in length from 2,000 to 8,000 words. Payment for cover features is $700 to $850; payment for inside features is $250 to $700. **Column pieces** run from 1,200 to 2,500 words in length. Topics include country life, city life, sports, dining, finance, arts, home gardening, and self-reliance. Payment is from $175 to $300. **Ohioana**: 50 to 800 word articles should be of solid news interest that other media missed or ignored. Looking for the "how" and "why" of stories as well as "what." Payment is from $50 to $50. **Ohioans**: 50 to 250 word pieces on Ohioans who are newsworthy -- event-makers and the offbeat. Payment is from $20 to $40. **Ohioguide**: 100 to 300 word articles on upcoming events. Must be worth traveling for. Payment is from $10 to $15. **Diner's Digest**: The editors are looking for writers with extensive restaurant reviewing experience to do 5 to 10 short reviews each month in specific sections of the state on a specific topic. Fee is on a retainer basis. Payment is made upon acceptance.

It is best to query first on all article ideas. For features and column ideas, query the Editor-in-Chief; for Ohioans and Ohioana, query the Managing Editor; and Diner's Digest and Ohio Guide, query the Copy Editor. With the query, especially the first time, the writer should send a selection of published clips.

Ohio buys all rights, but may reassign following publication rights: second serial (reprint), or one-time rights. The address of *Ohio* is 40 South Third Street, Columbus, Ohio 43215.

OKLAHOMA TODAY

Oklahoma Today, Official Magazine of the State of Ok-

lahoma - Bi-monthly magazine for people interested in reading about Oklahoma. Most articles are about travel and outdoor recreation, and occasionally, industry. Topics for possible freelance articles are: fishing, hiking, bicycling, museums, special events, lakes and parks, art, theater, music, sports, unusual restaurants and other attractions and activities. Topics though are not limited to these areas. People should be included with the topic -- either as participants in the activity, on the staff of the attraction, experts, or involved in some way. Article length should be 1,200 words. Query first. Include clippings of past published material with query. Payment rate is $100 and up and made upon acceptance.

Oklahoma Today informs people about interesting ways to spend their leisure time in Oklahoma. The criteria for most articles are: can the reader go see or participate in whatever the article is about; the history of an area or attraction may be woven into the background to add interest, but the emphasis should be on what can be seen today -- new trends, what people are doing, what is going on in the state. Preference will be given to less publicized activities or an unusual angle or fresh point of view on an old subject.

Address the Editor at *Oklahoma Today*, P. O. Box 53384, Oklahoma City, Oklahoma 73152-3384.

PHILADELPHIA MAGAZINE

Philadelphia Magazine - Monthly magazine. According to the Freelance Writer Guidelines, "It's tough to say what kind of stories we're looking for except that articles should make sense appearing in a magazine such as ours. So the best guide is the magazine itself -- prospective freelancers should read it regularly, or at least often enough to know what we do."

Freelance articles are accepted for four areas: features department, "Six Pages" and "Living Well". Regular department headings are: Crime, Business, City Journal, Politics, Making It, Exploits, Working, and Manners. Query the Articles Editor. *Philadelphia* also buys articles for the magazine's front-of-the-book "Six Pages" and back-of-the-book "Living Well" sections. With these, it is especially important that the writer know the format before querying. "Six Pages" items can run from one paragraph to 1,000 words, and proposals should be sent to the Associate Editor. Queries for

"Living Well" should go to the Living/Style Editor.

Payment is made upon acceptance: $500 for features, minimum of $200 for department articles, payment varies for articles in the "Six Pages" and "Living Well" sections.

First-time contributors should send clips of their published articles. Sample copies of *Philadelphia Magazine* are available by sending $3.00 to the Editorial Assistant. The address of *Philadelphia Magazine* is 1500 Walnut Street, Philadelphia, Pennsylvania 19102.

SAN ANTONIO MAGAZINE

San Antonio Magazine - Published monthly by the Greater San Antonio Chamber of Commerce. The purpose of the magazine is to tell the story of San Antonio, its businesses and its people, primarily for membership of the Greater San Antonio Chamber of Commerce, to the San Antonio community and to prospective businesses and industries.

Articles published in *San Antonio Magazine* deal with some aspect of local business or the general community. General features range from those about education, health, entertainment, the arts, sports and personalities to annual San Antonio events such as Fiesta and the Texas Open. Historical and travel pieces occasionally are run.

Major features and department highlights are needed. The average length of a major feature is 2,000 to 2,500 words, or 8 to 10 double-spaced pages. Department highlights are 500 to 750 words, or 2 to 3 double-spaced pages. Articles should be free of typographical and factual errors. It is the responsibility of the writer to double-check the spelling of persons, places, things and all figures before submitting the article.

Queries and unsolicited articles are acceptable. Queries should be as specific as possible and should be submitted in writing. Unsolicited articles should be considered to be submitted on speculation. Payment for an article is made upon acceptance and varies from $75 to $300 per article, depending on the length and complexity of the article.

Direct all correspondence to Editor, *San Antonio Magazine*, Post Office Box 1628, San Antonio, Texas 78296.

TEXAS HIGHWAYS MAGAZINE

Texas Highways Magazine, Official Travel Magazine for the State of Texas - This monthly needs articles on things to do or places to see in Texas. Include historical, cultural, and geographic aspects if appropriate. If you are writing about a place (a museum, amusement park, community or whatever), please send the editor the most descriptive folder or brochure. If you are writing about an event, then send the editor the most recent program. Length of article should be at least 500 words, or longer.

ACCURACY IS A MUST in spelling of names and quotes. Names and telephone numbers of all persons quoted or used as an information source for the article should be included with the manuscript. Articles are submitted on speculation only. Payment ranges from $150 to $600 ($.40 a word), depending on length. Pays upon acceptance. Query the Editor, *Texas Highways Magazine*, State Department of Highways and Public Transportation, Dewitt C. Greer State Highway Building, 11th and Brazos, Austin, Texas 78701-2843.

THE WASHINGTONIAN

The Washingtonian - Monthly city magazine which focuses almost exclusively on the Washington metropolitan area. The magazine was started in October 1965 and now has a circulation of over 135,000. Average household income of *The Washingtonian* subscriber is over $84,000 a year; median age is 40; and seven out of ten have finished college.

These types of freelance articles are sought: service pieces; profiles of people; investigative articles; rating pieces; institutional profiles; first-person articles; stories that cut across the grain of conventional thinking; articles that tell the reader how Washington got to be the way it is; light and satirical pieces (send the complete manuscript, the idea, because in this case, execution is everything). Subjects for articles include the federal government, local government, sports, business, education, medicine, fashion, environment, how to make money, how to spend money, real estate, performing arts, visual arts, travel, health, nightlife, hobbies, self-improvement, places to go, and things to do.

The editor is looking for three qualities in an article: thorough research and reporting, a writing style that is appropriate to the material, and the writer's ability to fit his/her material together and to give it meaning and focus.

The length of articles varies. Capital Comments range from 50 to 600 words; most front- and back-of-the-book pieces run 1,500 to 3,000 words; and center-of-the-book pieces are usually 2,000 to 7,000 words, but some run as long as 20,000 words.

Payment is $.20 to $.40 a word, depending on the length of the article, the amount of research, the number of interviews, and how much work the editor has to do on the article. One-third is paid upon acceptance of the manuscript and the remaining two-thirds on publication.

YANKEE MAGAZINE

Yankee Magazine is a monthly covering the New England region. Articles are needed on New England and/or New Englanders, past present or future; activities; controversies, if of wide interest; especially the unusual in all events; and historical, particularly if there is a present-day tie-in. Length of 1,500 to 2,500 words. Color transparencies of 35 mm, 2-1/4" x 2-1/4" or 4" x 5" are used with the above articles. Humor, folklore or legend material on New England is also wanted. Length up to 2,500 words.

Usually buys all rights. Payment ranges from $25 to $750 for full-length feature articles. With the higher payments, payment for photos is included.

Query first. The address is Editor, *Yankee Magazine*, Main Street, Dublin, New Hampshire 03444.

CHAPTER XVI

CAMPING AND RECREATIONAL VEHICLE PUBLICATIONS

Campers and motorhomes are other ways to travel. A number of publications are devoted to campers and motorhomes. Editors of these publications are looking for freelance material.

The following pages specify the types of articles wanted by editors of three publications: *Camping Today, Family Motor Coaching*, and *Trails-A-Way*. Why not investigate one or all three money-making opportunities? Again, they are listed alphabetically.

CAMPING TODAY

Camping Today - Published 12 times per years, this magazine serves 30,000 members of the National Campers and Hikers Association (NCHA) in the United States and Canada. *Camping Today* readers are owners of recreational vehicles such as camping trailers, travel trailers, fifth wheels, vans, motorhomes, and mini-motorhomes. They enjoy reading articles such as travel features, camping recipes, technical RV-related articles, and how-to features related to camping. A recent survey showed that travel pieces are enjoyed the best. Payment is in the range of $50 to $120, depending on length and type of article as well as photographs submitted. Payment is made upon publication, unless other arrangements are made. Submit completed article to the Editor at *Camping*

Today, 9425 S. Greenville Road, Greenville, Michigan 48838.

FAMILY MOTOR COACHING

Family Motor Coaching is the official monthly publication of the Family Motor Coach Association (FMCA). The magazines is geared to owners of motorhomes (not campers, trailers or other RVs).

Freelance material sought includes travel, technical, miscellaneous camp-related, FMCA-related articles, legal RV industry, coach reviews and profiles. Length of article varies except the length for travel articles should be 1,500 words.

Payment rates: standard travel article, $100 to $200; technical article, $100 to $300; coach review, $200 to $250; and all other, $50 to $200. Pays upon acceptance. Buys all rights.

Sample copies available for $2.00 apiece. Query the Editor at *Family Motor Coaching*, 8291 Clough Pike, Cincinnati, Ohio 45244.

TRAILS-A-WAY

Trails-A-Way - Newspaper published 11 times per year. Ten of those issues are divided into four separate editions reaching a combined circulation of 53,000 camping families in Michigan, Ohio, Indiana and Illinois. The 11th issue is the "Snowbird" edition which concentrates on the Sunbelt States but is distributed to the same Midwest readership. *Trail-A-Way* readers are owners of recreational vehicles and primarily interested in articles about places to go and things to do within this four state area.

Types of articles needed are: technical "how-to," camping recipes, favorite campgrounds, favorite camping trips, RV accessories, real-life camping humor, festivals, community celebrations, new RV and camping products, and test of new products.

Payment ranges from $75 to $125, depending on quality, length and photos. B/w glossy photos are preferred. Payment is made upon publication unless prior arrangements were made. Submit completed article to the Editor at *Trails-A-Way*, 9425 S. Greenville Road, Greenville, Michigan 48838.

CHAPTER XVII

SPORTS PUBLICATIONS

Sports publications are often in need of freelance material. A writer would have to have some knowledge of the sport in order to write for a certain publication. Overall, sports publications pay their writers excellent fees. The next pages contain a list of publications that accept freelance material. They are arranged alphabetically according to the sport and then by publication. For example, I have included publications on boating and sailing, bicycling and diving. There are 11 golden opportunities to sell your freelance work!

Backpacking
BACKPACKER

Backpacker - Bimonthly written and edited for the informed enthusiast, and for people just beginning to get involved in the sport. Major article categories are *how-to, where-to, and with what.* Approximately 60 to 70 percent of each issue deals with outdoor equipment, reflecting reader interest in knowing what is available that can make camping and hiking experiences easier and more rewarding. Technique and destination articles make up the bulk of the rest of each issue. Freelance articles are needed for the following areas: destination, weekend wilderness, materiel, first exposure, outfitting, geosphere, and body language. Length of articles varies. Read several issues of *Backpacker* to become acquainted with it.

Destination - Trip stories with emphasis on adventures readers can duplicate. Domestic destinations are preferred. 35 mm color transparency art is necessary. Interpret the trip -- plan and write about unusual occurrences, lessons learned, and discoveries not in guidebooks.

Weekend Wilderness - Short writeups on desirable hiking and camping destinations three hours or less from a metropolitan area.

Materiel - Discussion of a major component of backpacking equipment -- cordura, wool, synthetic insulations, and the like.

First Exposure - Wilderness photography tips.

Outfitting - Short roundup of a specific equipment category -- new bottled gas stoves, bivy socks, packs for cross-country ski-campers.

Geosphere - What can we learn from the earth; i.e., as hikers.

Body Language - Articles on health and conditioning are needed.

Payment for articles varies. Query the Editor at *Backpacking*, One Park Avenue, New York, New York 10016.

Bicycling
BICYCLING

Bicycling, America's Leading Cycling Magazine - Published nine times per year. Freelance articles are primarily needed on touring, notable cycling events, riding technique, and cycling in traffic. Typical length is 1,500 to 2,000 words but it can be 1,000 words to a maximum of 2,500 words.

Touring Features - Adventure or road-tested. Adventure tours are not intended to be how-to articles. They are first-person tales brought back from the rim of the world. Recently published articles focused on Iceland, Morocco, the Panamanian jungle, and the Sahara desert. Route information is unnecessary but writers should include anecdotes, suspense, a sensitive understanding of the local culture which you are visiting, some local history, the ability to make people in your story come alive and, of course, excellent photos.

Road-tested tours - Articles on these tours are published for other cyclists to try. Most tours are within the United States and Canada, but tours in any country *Bicycling* readers might like to visit will also be considered. In this type of article, include anecdotes, local cultures, route information, advice on where to camp (or rent a room), good restaurants, road conditions and the best time of year to tour.

Notable Cycling Events - Some cycling events deserve national recognition. Examples are: New York City's Five-Boro Bike Tour, San Diego's Five Cities Bike Tour and the Davis Double Century. In the writing, anecdotes, local color and a lively sense of the human beings involved will help to make your story readable. Film specs of 35 mm or 2-1/4" x 2-1/4"; shoot Kodachrome 64 or 25, if possible.

Bicycling buys all rights to articles and/or photographs, including the right to reuse in other Rodale Press publications, and the right to grant reprint permission, unless otherwise negotiated prior to publication. Query the Editor at *Bicycling*, 33 East Minor Street, Emmaus, Pennsylvania 18049.

VELO-NEWS

Velo-News, A Journal of Bicycle Racing - Written for very serious bicycle racing enthusiasts, *Velo-News'* readers are competitors, coaches, promoters and dedicated fans. They know bicycle racing well and expect high quality, detailed, expert writing on their favorite sport. The journal is published monthly from October through March and twice a month from April through September for a total of 18 issues each year.

Freelance features are needed on training, tactics, equipment, and race promoting as well as interviews with top riders or other personalities important to the sport. Length varies.

Minimum payment of $3 per column inch (about $13 per double-spaced, typed manuscript page). Photos may be included with the article. They should be 5" x 7" or 8" x 10" b/w prints. They should have borders and caption information should be included. Good photos are important.

Riding Technique - Articles may deal with the cyclist's efficiency on the bike or with interactions with other cyclists. These articles are frequently aimed at newer readers but certainly longtime readers can also benefit.

Cycling in Traffic - *Velo-News* editors seek to educate both newer and older readers in safe, predictable, and correct vehicle-like behavior in traffic with frequent articles on various in-traffic situations. Authors of these articles should have a good knowledge of traffic law and of the state of the art in bicycle safety training.

Photos will help to sell your article. Glossy b/w and color are acceptable. Minimum payment for photos is $15 each. If photos cover half a page or larger, a payment of $25 is made. *Velo-News* pays upon publication of articles and photos.

Query the Editor at *Velo-News*, Box 1257, Brattleboro, Vermont 05301.

Boating and Sailing

LAKELAND BOATING

Lakeland Boating - Monthly magazine devoted to boating enthusiasts throughout the Great Lakes and northern central states. Geographic areas of primary readership include: Illinois, Indiana, Michigan, Minnesota, New York, Ohio, Pennsylvania, Wisconsin, surrounding Midwest states and Southern Ontario and Southern Quebec provinces in Canada. Nearly 80% of its readers own a powerboat of some type: the majority of which are 19-feet or more in length. And 20% of its readers own a sailboat. Because of this ratio of powerboaters to sailors, *Lakeland Boating* skews more editorials toward powerboating or prefers articles which apply to boaters of all types.

Freelance articles are needed in the following areas: port o'call, weekender, technical, historical and environmental. **Port-o'Call** - Long distance cruising features deal with Great Lakes ports only; good, clear photos with manuscript. **Weekender** - Short cruising features generally on inland lakes and rivers; submit good, clear photos with article. **Technical** - Boat and engine maintenance, trailering, safety, new gear, weather, boat handling, electronics. **Historical** - Articles dealing with boating and the Great Lakes -- shipwrecks, treasure hunting, explorers, naval battles are sought.

Submit only color transparencies or b/w photos; no color prints. Payment is upon publication, $.10 to $20 per word, including photos.

Query the Editor first with published clips. The address is *Lakeland Boating*, 505 N. Lakeshore Drive, Suite 5704, Chicago, Illinois 60611. A sample copy is $2.

MOTOR BOATING AND SAILING

Motor Boating and Sailing - Monthly covering powerboats and sailboats for people who own their own boats and are active in a yachting lifestyle. Circulation is 140,000.

The editors are looking for general interest and how-to articles. General interest deals with navigation, adventure and cruising. How-to deals with maintenance. Length of 2,000 words. Photos are accepted with articles but there is no additional payment. These types and sizes are wanted: 5" x 7" glossy b/w prints and 35 mm or larger color transparencies.

Payment varies and is upon acceptance. Buys one-time rights. Query the Editor at *Motor Boating and Sailing*, 224 W. 57th Street, New York, New York 10019.

SAIL

Sail - Monthly written and edited for everyone who sails-- aboard a one-design boat or an offshore racer, a day sailer or an auxiliary cruiser.

Freelance material is needed for four areas: features; how-to, technical; side features; and news. **Features** - Writers should focus on a theme or some aspect of sailing and discuss a personal attitude or new philosophical approach to the subject. Certain issues are devoted to special themes. For instance, the March issue has frequently featured chartering, and the January or February issue, the Southern Ocean Racing Conference. These are not definite or fixed topics but will give the writer an idea of the magazine's schedule. Length of 1,500 to 3,500 words. **How-to, technical** - Clear, concise articles directed to the intelligent layman are sought. The writer should discuss systems or techniques for navigation, sail trim, or seamanship that have worked well for him/her. Technical articles should describe the successful methods of approaching projects or concepts of sailing, not bemoan unsuccessful ways. Deal with one subject in detail, rather than cover a wide range of topics superficially. Length should be 1,500 to 3,500 words.

Side Features - Short articles of 1,000 to 1,500 words run the gamut from vignettes of day sailing, cruising, and racing life, at home or abroad, straight or humorous, to accounts of maritime history, astronomy, marine life, cooking aboard, nautical lore, and fishing, to miscellaneous pieces about boat owning, building and outfitting. How-to pieces should be specific and instructive. They should sharply focus on a single theme of broad interest to sailors and, if appropriate, should be illustrated by anecdotes from your personal experience. **News** - News reporting is usually assigned in advance. Query the Sail Editor at least one month prior to the event you are interested in covering. News reporting must be accurate and clear. Regatta sports should include a copy of the official score sheet and the names, home cities, and final score of the top 10 finishers. Be sure to describe the number and type of boats competing, the weather, and the general racing action. Advance queries about non-racing events are always welcome.

Payment for articles varies. The address of *Sail* is Charlestown Navy Yard, 100 First Avenue, Charlestown, Massachusetts 02129-2097.

SOUNDINGS

Soundings, The Nation's Boating Newspaper is the only national boating newspaper in the country. It is a monthly covering five geographic areas. Freelance material is needed for the following departments: Editorial, Galley Muse, Offshore Beat, Power Play, Reflections, Working Water's Edge, Fishing, Keeping Current, Legislative News, Marine Heritage, Race Results, Sail Tracks and Waterfront Watch. Length for news articles should be limited to 250 to 750 words, features should not exceed 1,000 words.

Article payment is $2 a published inch, sometimes higher. Payment of $15 minimum for 8" x 10" b/w glossy prints. Payment is made upon publication, on the 10th of the month of publication.

Buys one-time rights. Send complete manuscripts to *Soundings*, Essex, Connecticut 06426.

SOUTHERN BOATING

Southern Boating, the South's Largest Boating Magazine-Monthly publishes articles of interest to power and sailing yachtsmen in areas covering southeastern coastal waters (not inland) from the Carolinas to Texas, including the Bahamas and the Caribbean. Distribution is by subscription, newsstand, and as part of the inflight library on all Eastern, Air Florida, and Capitol Airlines flights.

Editorially, the magazine focuses on the pleasure derived from boating with family and friends. Typical subjects of interest to readers include cruising by power or sail (where to go, what to do, how to get there), provisioning, do-it-yourself maintenance and repair, how-to ideas, safety tips, navigation, sportfishing, and major boating competition.

Articles should run from 1,000 to 2,500 words. Authors should supply supporting artwork or photos.

Payment ranges from $50 to $100 per article/photo-art depending upon length, overall quality and amount of art/photos. Query the Editor at *Southern Boating*, 1975 N.W. South River Drive, Miami, Florida 33125.

TRAILER BOATS MAGAZINE

Trailer Boats Magazine is a monthly except for a combined November/December issue. It is edited for those who own or plan to purchase a craft normally trailered behind the family car or truck.

Various types of freelance articles are needed: articles describing trailer boating activities such as boat club outings; humor; tips and instructions on how to repair boats or motors, install equipment or handle other projects; nostalgia and historical material related to places, events or boats; stories about boating travel on water or highways; and profile, personal experience, photo features and technical articles. Length varies.

Trailer Boats Magazine is a visually oriented magazine and uses photos virtually with every article. Submit 5" x 7" or 8" x 10" size glossy b/w prints or color transparencies. Additional payment for photos is made.

Article payment ranges from $.07 to $.10 per word upon publication. Buys all rights.

Query the Editor at *Trailer Boats Magazine*, Poole Publications, Inc., 16427 S. Avalon, P. O. Box 2307, Gardena, California 90247-0307.

Bowling

THE WOMAN BOWLER

The Woman Bowler - Official publication of the Women's International Bowling Congress (WIBC). Founded in 1936, it is published 11 times each year, with a combined issue in July-August. Current circulation is 155,000. The magazine is mailed to individual subscribers, the secretary of every WIBC sanctioned winter league (women's and mixed), bowling proprietors, news medial personnel, bowling officials and a selected group of advertisers.

The purpose of *The Woman Bowler* is to provide information of interest to women bowlers, including articles about

WIBC services, rules and plans, high scoring women bowlers, league and tournament activities, ideas and instructional information and complete coverage of the WIBC Championship Tournament and Annual Meeting.

Writers should keep these three things in mind when submitting article ideas. First, *The Woman Bowler* is a national magazine whose readership encompasses WIBC's more than four million members in more than 165,000 leagues in nearly 2,700 local associations in every state. Second, articles are selected for publication on the basis of general interest to readers and/or national significance. Third, there re thousands of triple scores, all-spare games, and split conversions among members each season. Unless there is some unusual angle, it is not possible to use articles about such accomplishments.

Specifically, these types of freelance articles are needed: "Did You Hear About" (feature accomplishments by the lower or medium-average women bowlers); "Senior Scenes"; "Times to Celebrate"; letters from readers; articles about high score games (300, 299, 298) and series (700s and 800s); human interest and feature angles; different league or tournament ideas; humorous or unusual happenings; and hints on banquet plans. Length of articles varies.

Query the Editor at *The Woman Bowler*, Women's International Bowling Congress, 5301 South 76th Street, Greendale, Wisconsin 53129.

Diving

UNDERCURRENT

Undercurrent, The Private Exclusive Guide for Serious Divers - Monthly newsletter for experienced scuba divers. *Undercurrent* is a consumer review; its staff are critics and judges; they uncover problems in the industry and write about them. The more investigative an article is, the more likely the editors are interested in it. Because of the specific style, freelance articles are usually rewritten.

Freelance articles are needed on equipment, saving money, safety, training and other topics. Articles should be factual, to the point and analytical. Length varies.

Payment is $.08 to $.10 per word, payable upon publication. Query the Editor at *Undercurrent*, P. O. Box 1658, Sausalito, California 94965.

CHAPTER XVIII

MORE SPORTS PUBLICATIONS

This chapter is a continuation of the previous chapter. The publications are listed alphabetically by sport and then listed alphabetically under each category of sport. Fishing, hockey and martial arts are some of the categories. In all, there are 29 moneymaking opportunities for your freelance work.

Fishing

THE FLYFISHER
The Flyfisher - Quarterly official publication of the Federation of Fly Fishers, a non-profit organization of 10,000 individual members and 250 member clubs around the world. Three types of freelance articles are needed: how-to, where to go, and angling literature and tradition.
How-to - New wrinkles in fly fishing and tackle, including knots, splices, rod-making, fly tying and fishing techniques. This type of article must be well illustrated with photos or artwork.
Where to go - Places of interest to fly fishermen, be it quality waters with "catch and release" regulations, or less known waters which can provide a pleasant day of fishing. This type of article should let the reader know what type of patterns to use and how the different seasons of the year affect the fishing. There must be more value to the story than that of a simple travelogue.

Angling literature and tradition - Articles are needed on the development of fly fishing, including profiles of angling pioneers, stories on the development of historic fly patterns, histories of famous angling clubs or lodges, analysis of angling literature, and collecting of historic angling objects.

Length of articles varies from 500 to 2,500 words. The preferred length is 500 to 1,000 words.

Good photographs are essential in the acceptance of most articles. B/w 8" x 10" glossy prints should accompany all articles, since the majority of the pages will be one color or two color pages. Good color transparencies (35 mm, 2-1/4" x 2-1/4" or 4" x 5") may also accompany any submitted article. If you have b/w negatives, but no access to producing 8" x 10" prints, send in the negatives and what prints you have. *The Flyfisher* staff makes the prints it needs.

Payment ranges from $50 to $200 for article-photo packages. Payment follows publication.

Sample copies of *The Flyfisher* are available by sending $3 to Federation of Fly Fishers, P. O. Box 1088, West Yellowstone, Montana 59758. Query the Editor at *The Flyfisher*, 1387 Cambridge Drive, Idaho Falls, Idaho 83401.

GREAT LAKES FISHERMAN

Great Lakes Fisherman - Monthly which covers all phases of angling in New York, Pennsylvania, Ohio, Michigan, Indiana, Illinois, Wisconsin and Minnesota. Coverage is not limited to the fish and fishing within waters of the five Great Lakes, but extends region-wide, and includes all warm and coldwater game and panfish species. Reports on tributary streams, inland lakes and in shore. Besides freelance articles on fishing, technical, scientific, humor, interview and profile type articles are needed. Preferred length is from 1,500 to 2,000 words.

Payment is $125 to $200 for article/photo package; good 5" x 7" or 8" x 10" b/w photos are sought. Pays upon publication. Buys one-time rights. Query the Editor at *Great Lakes Fisherman*, Great Lakes Fisherman Publishing Co., Inc., P. O. Box 20286, Columbus, Ohio 43220.

OHIO FISHERMAN

Ohio Fisherman - Monthly devoted to Ohio fishermen. Needs fishing articles -- how to fish, where to fish and when to fish. Interviews, profiles, scientific, historical and humorous pieces are also sought. Length should be 1,500 to 2,000 words.

Payment is $75 to $125 including photos. Good 5" x 7" or 8" x 10" b/w enlargements are needed. All photos must be captioned and depict Ohio fishing. Pays upon publication. Buys one-time rights.

Query the Editor at *Ohio Fisherman*, Ohio Fisherman Publishing Co., Inc., P. O. Box 20096, Columbus, Ohio 43220.

SALT WATER SPORTSMAN (R)

Salt Water Sportsman (R) - Monthly dealing with marine sport fishing along the coasts of the United States and Canada, the Caribbean, Central America, Bermuda and occasionally South America, and overseas areas.

Two types of articles are needed: features and material for the "Sportsman's Workbench" department. Buys First American Rights. **Features** - Emphasis should be on how-to of salt water fishing, not straight "Me & Joe" adventures. Specific semi-technical information that the average reader will understand is sought. Articles dealing with angling at a specific time of year should be submitted about six months ahead of the optimum publication date, and no less than four months at minimum. Articles should be 1,500 to 1,800 words. Features with photos are purchased as a package.

A good selection of 8" x 10" bordered, b/w glossy prints and 35 mm Kodachrome transparencies should be submitted. Manuscript/photos are bought as a package. The average payment rate runs from $200 to $275, but may be more if copy is clean and photos are above average. Pays upon acceptance. For features, query the Editor at *Salt Water Sportsman*, 186 Lincoln Street, Boston, Massachusetts 02111. **"Sportsman's Workbench"** - Freelance articles are needed for this department. They should be 100 to 1,000 word, how-to articles dealing with all phases of salt water fishing, tackle, boats and related equipment. Emphasis is on building, repairing or reconditioning specific items of gear, creating new rigs, or any new ideas that may appeal to *Salt Water Sportsman* readers. Rough or finish artwork and/or b/w photos may accompany copy and will influence rates paid. Rates vary as to length and amount of illustration. *No query is necessary.* Submit material to the Managing Editor, *Salt Water Sportsman*, 186 Lincoln Street, Boston, Massachusetts 02111.

When submitting photos, 8" x 10", b/w bordered glossy

prints and 35 mm Kodachrome transparencies are wanted. They should show action and be scenic. There should be a good selection and a mix of vertical and horizontal shots.

TEXAS FISHERMAN

Texas Fisherman, A Complete Guide To The Texas Outdoors - Published monthly, except bi-monthly in July/August, September/October and November/December.

Three types of freelance articles are needed: location, product and technique. **Feature articles** - Cover fishing hotspots which could be recently built, relatively unexplored lakes, or, on the other hand, places that have been there for years that deserve due recognition because of the angling opportunities that they offer. The article should include the seasonal tendencies of the area, which locations are productive at what time of the year, and how the fish should be approached during that season. **Product stories** - Items dealt with should not only be new, but also practical for the consumer. Both the advantages and disadvantages of such products should be brought out, explained through not only the writer's own experiences, but also the comments of experts within the industry. **Technique articles** - This type of article focuses on the newest fishing techniques. Many of these methods are developed by fishing guides, tournament fishermen, field testers, and occasionally, long-time "average-Joe" fishermen who come across a new way to use traditional equipment. All of these people are potential contacts for fresh story material. Whether they are the source of a full-fledged interview or simply provide the writer with additional information, their techniques are an important asset to a story concerning technique.

Eight to ten double-spaced pages is the norm for the length. All articles should have b/w photos; 8" x 10" size is preferred but 5" x 7" size will be accepted. Payment ranges from $150 to $200, depending upon length and quality of photos. Query the Editor at *Texas Fisherman*, 5314 Bingle Road, Houston, Texas 77092.

WASHINGTON FISHING HOLES

Washington Fishing Holes - Monthly publication for Washington anglers, featuring subjects within the state. Occasionally publishes a travel or vacation fishing piece in a nearby state or province, slanted to the traveling Washington angler.

Three types of freelance articles are sought: where-to-go, how-to-do-it and techniques.

Where-to-go features - These articles focus on all types of fishing and any species of fish, anywhere in the state, from the ocean to high mountain lakes, major rivers to desert creeks. The area must be open to the public and capable of sustaining the potential fishing pressure that may be generated by publicity. The featured area should have a slant that makes it special... spectacular scenery, good camping, a special strain of fish, or above-average size fish. When you are writing, use good quotes which add spice and local knowhow. Talk with local resort operators, other anglers, the local "expert", regional fish biologist or game warden. Concentrate on a specific season, but add a few paragraphs describing the area's potential during the rest of the year. Fishing maps should be part of the where-to-go features. Include these things on the map: the depths, fishing areas, landmarks, facilities, pertinent structure, boat launches, resort, nearby roads, a scale (in feet, miles or meters) and a compass bearing. Maps should be drawn; ideally, seven inches wide and no more than 10 inches high, or 4-5/8 inches wide and no more than 10 inches high, depending upon the configuration of the mapped areas. All maps are redrawn by the staff artist and artistic achievement, though welcome, is not as critical as detail and legibility. Check all local spellings, against state map spellings. **How-to-do-it features** - These articles concentrate on new techniques, improvements in old techniques, and making lures. The editors are always on the lookout for fresh, new ideas or different approaches. Examples are getting the most out of your downrigger, modify your lures and go deep for big bottomfish. Line art and illustrations plus photos are essential to how-to pieces. **Technique articles** - These articles describe in detail local fishing techniques, including rod models, reels, pound test line, weights and lures. For example, if there is a specialized or complicated, out-of-the-ordinary rigging, include a diagram of it, spelling out exact measurements and dimensions. Get down to the "nitty-gritty" on techniques, and line stripping. An illustration of the best lures (drawn or photographed), flies or bait is valuable. In short, put the reader in the right place, at the right time of year, using the right lures or baits, with the right technique.

Photos will help sell your article. They can be 5" x 7" or 8" x 10" b/w glossies or 35 mm transparencies (ASA 64 or slower). They should show action, be scenic and close-ups of fish. The editors want a selection of 6 to 12 photos from which to choose.

Average payment is $105, based on $75 per feature and $15 for each photo or illustration published. Buys first and second publication rights. Second time rights non-exclusive. Photos need not be first-time rights.

Query the Editor at *Washington Fishing Holes*, 114 Avenue C, Snohomish, Washington 98290.

GAME & FISH PUBLICATIONS

Game & Fish Publications, Inc. publishes a number of monthly magazines. They are:
Georgia Sportsman
Texas Sportsman
Florida Game & Fish
Carolina Game & Fish
Missouri Game & Fish
Virginia - West Virginia Game & Fish
Louisiana Game & Fish
Alabama Game & Fish
Oklahoma Game & Fish
Tennessee Sportsman
Kentucky Game & Fish
Arkansas Sportsman
Mississippi Game & Fish

A sample copy is $2.50. Request the specific magazine(s). The address is Game & Fish Publications, Inc., P. O. Box 741, Marietta, Georgia 30061.

All publications are information-oriented magazines with a focus on hunting, fishing, and outdoor recreation related to hunting and fishing in each state of publication. Length should be from 2,200 to 2,400 words. Emphasis is on how-to, when-to, where-to, or true adventure stories. Also, articles dealing with major legislation or environmental issues affecting the respective states are desired.

Articles fall into two basic categories, state-specific and combo. State-specific articles are those written specifically for a particular state or a region within that state. Combo articles are those that are written to apply to the entire coverage area. Standard payment rates for published articles are as follows: State-specific (published in one magazine), $150; Combo (published in two or more state magazines), $250. Payment is made on the 15th day of the month three months prior to the cover date of the magazine(s) the article appears in.

Photography and/or charts, graphs, maps, and illustrations complementing an article are considered extremely important. Color transparencies, preferably kodachrome, and b/w 8" x 10" glossy prints are needed. Photos should depict prominently the species involved with the appropriate background for each state. Additional payment is made for photos. Payment varies.

Game & Fish Publications buy one-time rights on articles and photos. Query with your article idea to the Editor of the specific magazine.

Guns
GUNS MAGAZINE

Guns Magazine is published monthly. Text/photo packages are sought. Articles can be on hunting, test reports, round-ups, think pieces, and historical pieces. Length varies. Photos should be b/w Kodak Tri-X, 5" x 7" or 8" x 10" prints, or Kodak Ektachrome 200 ASA color transparencies. If you have larger size color transparencies, 2-1/4" x 2-1/4" or 3" x 5", they are also welcome.

Buys first North American serial rights. Payment rates are: $75 to $500 for articles, $175 for columns, and $25 for book reviews (per book).

Query the Editor at *Guns Magazine*, 591 Camino de la Reina, Suite 200, San Diego, California 92108.

Hockey
AMERICAN HOCKEY MAGAZINE

American Hockey Magazine - Published seven times annually by the Amateur Hockey Association of the United States. According to the writers' guidelines, it is "America's Only Amateur Hockey Magazine." It is a mainly controlled-circulation publication, distributed to amateur hockey enthusiasts in the United States.

Human interest features, as well as stories relating to one of these departments are needed: Americans in the Pros, College Notes, Rink and Arenas, For the Record, Coach's Playbook, and Referee's Crease.

Authors are paid $150 for a 2,000 word feature and $75 for 1,000 word department article. Buys first-time, North American rights.

Query the Managing Editor at *American Hockey Magazine*, 2997 Broadmoor Valley Road, Colorado Springs, Colorado 80906.

Hunting and Fishing
GRAY'S SPORTING JOURNAL

Gray's Sporting Journal - Quarterly published in February, May, August and November. The issues are devoted to the following subjects: February, hunting and fishing, evenly mixed; May, fishing primarily; August, hunting and fishing, with a slight bias toward bird hunting; and November, hunting primarily. Freelance material is sought for three sections: features, yarnspin and Gray's Current.

Features - These make up the bulk of each issue, and five to ten are bought each time. They can be as short as 1,000 words. The median is 3,000 words. Features can be submitted with or without photos. Additional payment is made for photos. If you have a good story and no photos, please submit it -- the publication's sources are good and *Gray's Sporting Journal* can find the photos. Payment ranges from $500 to $1,000.

Yarnspin - These are short yarns, unadorned. What is needed here is humor, history, anecdote, prevarication-- whatever you wish to submit. Any length from a paragraph to 1,500 words; preferably 250 to 500 words. Writing standards in this section are nonexistent: the editors do not care that you cannot spell if the story is entertaining. Yarnspins should be told in a conversational, or letter-writing mode, and can be colloquial. A good, secondhand tale, well repeated, is fine. Payment is $100 or $200, depending on length.

Gray's Current - This section is the newsletter. It includes current news, both hard and soft, letters to the editor, reviews of books and articles, and a section called "Need We Say More?" in which things are reproduced that were found in print and strike the editors as particularly outrageous or funny, and are, therefore, worth reproducing without comment. Payment is $50.

Buys first-time Northern American serial rights. A sample copy is $5. Query the Editor at *Gray's Sporting Journal*, 205 Willow Street, P. O. Box 2549, South Hamilton, Massachusetts

01982.

Hunting Only

BOWHUNTER (R)

Bowhunter (R), The Magazine for the Hunting Archer- Published seven times a year by Blue-J, Inc. Special interest publication written for, by and about bowhunters. *Bowhunter's* purpose is to both entertain and inform readers. How-to-do-it and where-to-go articles are always in demand. Many of the magazine's contributors simply have an interesting tale to share. Some conservation and humorous articles are also bought. All articles should include information on equipment, seasons, outfitters, and costs -- things that help the reader picture the situation and might enable him/her to duplicate the experience.

Filler pieces are usually a few hundred words and long features can go up to 5,000 words. The average feature runs 2,500 words. Payment begins at $25 and runs to $250, possibly more. Average payment is $75 to $150. Buys first North American serial rights only. Photos are usually purchased with the article -- b/w 5" x 7" or 8" x 10" glossy prints, color 2-1/4" x 2-1/4" or 35 mm transparencies.

Query the Editor/Publisher at *Bowhunter*, 3150 Mallard Cover Lane, Fort Wayne, Indiana 46804.

TURKEY CALL

Turkey Call - Official bimonthly educational publication of the National Wild Turkey Federation, Inc. The National Wild Turkey Foundation, Inc. is a nonprofit membership organization dedicated to the wise conservation and management of the American Wild Turkey as a valuable natural resource.

Three types of freelance articles are wanted: feature articles of 1,500 to 2,000 words, short items and illustrated materials. **Features** - Can deal with the history, restoration, management, biology, distribution, and hunting of the American Wild Turkey. "How-to" and "where-to-go" articles and those giving a fresh treatment to familiar themes are also needed. Familiar themes include: "how the wild turkey disappeared and was later successfully reintroduced in my state or region," and "how I bagged my first gobbler." *Turkey Call* readers know this subject and writers must deal "expertly" with it. Photos are usually purchased with articles as a package. B/w 8" x 10" glossy prints and any size transparencies are needed. They should be action and scenic shots shot closeup, medium and long distances with high, low and wide angles. The broader the photo selection, the better.

Payment ranges from $25 for short items, to $50 for short articles of a few hundred words, up to $275 for an illustrated feature. Payment is usually upon publication but sometimes can be made upon acceptance.

Queries are appreciated but not necessary. The address is Editor, *Turkey Call*, P. O. Box 530, Edgefield, South Carolina 29824.

WATERFOWLER'S WORLD

Waterfowler's World - Bimonthly for serious duck and goose hunters who are keenly interested in improving their skills. Accurate and tightly written articles are a must. Read the magazine first before submitting an article idea. A sample copy is $2.50.

Article needs vary; the best source is the magazine itself. Length and payment also vary. A selection of b/w glossy prints and several color slides should accompany all articles.

Query first with published works to the Editor at *Waterfowler's World*, P. O. Box 38306, Germantown, Tennessee 38138.

Martial Arts
INSIDE KUNG FU

Inside Kung Fu - Monthly which needs a variety of feature articles, 8 to 10 typewritten pages. Types of articles sought are: training stories, traditional articles, technical articles, historical articles, self-defense stories, evolution columns, travel stories, mass media stories, personality profile/interview articles, philosophy, and health.

Training stories - Articles about new or unique ways of training, often tailored to a certain type of development. **Traditional articles** - Focus on little-known arts and styles. Traditional articles discuss the history, combat theories, and training practices of an art. They may also cover the lifestyle of the arts' practitioners. **Historical articles** - Articles that trace the origin and history of a style or group of styles, or the life of a great martial artist from the past. **Self-defense stories** - Articles that present specific methods and/or tactics that are applicable to street self-defense. **Evolution columns** - Short (1,000 words) think pieces, provocative or controversial viewpoints on any martial arts topic.

Travel stories - Articles about martial arts styles, traditions, and masters in a foreign country. High-quality photos are essential for this type of story. **Mass media stories** - A limited number of features on martial arts and martial artists in the movie industry, both in the U. S. and Hong Kong, are accepted. **Personality profile/interview articles** - Articles of this type should deal with individuals who are well known to the entire martial arts world, such as Ed Parker and Chuck Norris. **Philosophy** - These articles deal with the relationship of Zen, Taoism, or other Asian philosophies to the martial arts. **Health** - These stories discuss any aspect of health, including diet, preventing injuries, treating injuries, Chinese medical practices, specifically aimed at the martial artist and his/her needs.

Photos should be submitted with articles either as 8" x 10" b/w glossies, as negatives with contact sheets, or the entire roll of film may be sent in to be developed by the magazine. 35 mm (or larger) format camera sizes are preferred; snapshots are nearly useless to the magazine.

Payment is made upon publication. The payment schedule is as follows: 10-page feature article with photographs, $100 to $125; 10-page feature article without photos, $75 to $100; and columns (about 1,000 words), $35. Query the Editor at *Inside Kung Fu*, 4201 W. Vanowen Place, Burbank, California 91505.

Outdoors
FIELD & STREAM (TM)

Field & Stream (TM), America's No. 1 Sportsman's Magazine - Monthly, broad-based outdoor service magazine. Freelance material is needed for features, "How It's Done" and "Did You Know?" The key word is *service*. The "Me and Joe" story rarely works, with the exception of well-written adventure articles. On the whole, article-photo packages are bought.

Features of 2,000 to 2,500 words are sought. They can be on such subjects as national conservation; game management; resource management issues; recreational hunting, fishing; travel nature; and outdoor equipment. Payment ranges from $500 to four figures, depending on the experience of the author and the quality of his/her work. **How It's Done** articles of 500 to 900 words tell in pictures (or drawings) and words how an outdoor technique is accomplished or device is made. Payment is $250. **"Did You Know"** articles are of three lengths -- 300 words, 550 words, and 700 words. Payment is made upon acceptance.

Field & Stream buys First World Rights but returns the rights to the author after publication. A sample copy is $1.95. Query the Editor at *Field & Stream*, 1515 Broadway, New York, New York 10036.

MICHIGAN OUT-OF-DOORS

Michigan Out-Of-Doors - Monthly established in 1947 by the Michigan United Conservation Clubs (MUCC), the nation's largest state conservation organization. Circulation is approximately 110,000. The magazine's areas of interest are: outdoor recreation, with special emphasis on hunting and fishing; conservation; and environmental affairs.

Freelance articles should have a Michigan setting, although material of general interest is sometimes purchased. These types of articles are wanted: full-length features of up to 2,000 words; "how-to, when-to, where-to" articles; documented investigative pieces; personal adventure and nature-lore essays. Payment for full-length features with photos ranges from $75 to $150. Payment for other articles varies. Payment is made upon acceptance.

Query the Editor at *Michigan Out-of-Doors*, Michigan United Conservation Clubs, 2101 Wood Street, P. O. Box 30235, Lansing, Michigan 48909.

WESTERN OUTDOORS (R)

Western Outdoors (R) is the News Magazine for the Western Sportsman - It covers hunting, fishing and related recreational activities in the 11 contiguous Western States, Alaska, Hawaii, Western Canada, Mexico's West Coast and Baja California. It is published 10 times per year, combining December-January and July-August as the "outlook" and "Fall Preview" issues.

The editors are looking for **news features** which are defined as articles written in the third person, preferably with a news angle, and with the writer as reporter. Instead of first-person, personal experience stories, *Western Outdoors (R)* seeks articles which are well-researched and quote authoritative sources of information. For example, those sources could be experienced guides or outfitters, veteran sportsmen, concessionaires, resort operators, longtime local residents, government officials, agency personnel -- persons whom the reader will perceive to be authorities on the subject. News angles can be anything as uncomplicated as the opening of a new fishing or hunting area to something as potentially complex as a controversial issue or situation affecting sportsmen.

If you want to be published in *Western Outdoors (R)*, submit a news feature of 1,200 to 1,500 words with a news angle, describing a place to go in the West for a pleasurable experience and a reasonable chance of success in hunting or fishing; a sidebar of about 250 words on how to do it once there; and a "Trip Facts" sidebar telling: "How to Get There," "Where To Stay," "Best Seasons," "Approximate Costs" and "Whom To Contact," in that order. The package should also include a map of the area, either hand-drawn or a local road map, for use by the cartographer, and -- most importantly -- excellent color transparencies.

Western Outdoors (R) buys first North American serial rights only. Payment is made upon acceptance. The usual rate is $250 to $300, depending upon the quality of writing and photography, the amount of editing and rewriting necessary, and other facts as determined by the editor.

Sample copies are available at many newsstands or can be obtained by sending $1.50 handling cost to *Western Outdoors (R)*. Established writers are eligible for half-price subscriptions.

Query the Editor about your article idea at *Western Outdoors (R)*, 3197-E Airport Loop Drive, Costa Mesa, California 92626.

CHAPTER XIX

HOBBY AND CRAFT PUBLICATIONS

Another type of market which freelance writers might like to sell to is hobby and craft. There re publications for the beginner as well as the experienced hobbyist/craftsperson. On the whole, payment for articles is quite good.

Many of these publications are looking for how-to articles which give detailed instructions on how-to make something or do something. I have arranged the publications alphabetically so the reader can go to the craft or hobby he or she is most interested in. I have also alphabetized the publications under the categories for the reader's convenience.

Antiques and Collecting

ANTIQUE REVIEW

Antique Review - Monthly tabloid whose editors are interested in receiving material about antiques in America prior to 1880, the craftspersons who produced them, and their current status in the antiques marketplace. Articles should be from 700 to 2,500 words with quality 3" x 5" glossy b/w photos.

Payment is from $80 to $100, usually at the time of publication. If an article is accepted for publication for a future but unspecified issue, payment will be made upon acceptance. *Antique Review* prefers to have first Northern American serial rights but will consider articles which have been published in non-antique periodicals such as in city newspapers, historical society newsletters, doctoral thesis and subject-oriented publications. In all cases, *Antique Review* is interested in one time and reprint rights and will be happy to reassign rights to the author following first publication.

Query the Editor at *Antique Review*, P.O. Box 538, Worthington, Ohio 43085.

THE ANTIQUE TRADER WEEKLY

The Antique Trader Weekly, "America's Widest Used Publication on Antiques & Collector's Items." - Published 52 weeks a year, this tabloid newspaper contains informative articles, show and auction reports, calendar of events, classified and display ads from dealers and collectors across the nation. Collectors and dealers consider it the "bible" of the hobby.

Two types of freelance articles are needed: inside feature and cover feature. They should be well researched and can be on all types of antiques and collectors' items. The preferred length is 1,000 to 2,000 words. **Inside features** - should have a generous amount of b/w photos. Payment is from $5 to $50. **Cover features** - should have a 4" x 5" color transparency or slide for the cover (sometimes a smaller transparency or slide is acceptable) and several b/w photos to illustrate the inside text. Payment is generally from $150 to $200.

When an article is accepted for use in *The Antique Trader Weekly*, the author is notified of the amount of payment which will be made after publication of the article and then is asked to fill out and return a brief contract which grants the publication complete Northern American rights on that article. Payment is made at the end of the month, or, more usually, at the beginning of the month following publication. Only cover features and seasonal material can be tentatively scheduled for use. Other articles are used on a "space available" basis and several months may elapse between acceptance and publication of an article. Articles may also be reprinted in one of the other Babka Publishing Co. publications.

Send complete manuscripts to The Editorial Department, *The Antique Trader Weekly*, P. O. Box 1050, Dubuque, Iowa 52001.

COLLECTOR EDITIONS

Collector Editions is a quarterly consumer journal dealing with limited edition collectibles, ceramics and glass. Most first articles are written on speculation. The collecting angle should be stressed in the articles. Possible ideas for articles are contemporary (post-war) collectibles, including reproductions, antiques that are being reproduced today and generally available, and profiles of celebrity collectors. Article length ranges from 500 to 2,000 words with the majority of articles published being under 1,000 words. Submit b/w or color photos with manuscript but there is no additional payment. Payment is up to $350 and upon publication.

Sample copies are available for $1 each. Query the Editor at *Collector Editions*, Collector Communications Corp., 170 Fifth Avenue, New York, New York 10010.

COLLECTORS NEWS & THE ANTIQUE REPORTER

Collectors News & The Antique Reporter - Monthly tabloid newspaper which accepts freelance articles on glass and china, toys, music and records, furniture, art, dolls, transportation, bottles, timepieces, jewelry, lamps, valentines, political items, and any other collectibles, antiques and timely subjects. Articles about people's collections are also welcome. Length should be 2,000 words or less.

B/w photos, preferably glossy, should accompany the article. Sometimes b/w snapshots of good quality with plenty of dark and light contrast and suitable for newsprint reproduction can be used.

Front page features utilizing full color pictures are also needed. They should be arranged four months in advance to allow for necessary processing and avoidance of conflict in scheduling. All inquiries on color picture articles should be accompanied by a short but informative summary of the article's content.

Basic payment is $.75 per column inch, including space required for photos. Major front page articles are paid for at a higher rate. Payment is normally made upon publication.

Query the Editor at *Collectors News & The Antique Reporter*, P. O. Box 156, Grundy Center, Iowa 50638.

EARLY AMERICAN LIFE

Early American Life - Monthly which combines elements of history, antiques collecting, home decorating, food, travel, architecture, hobbies, arts and crafts into a final product that is designed to help readers bring something of the warmth and beauty of early America into their lives. The publication has a bit of the personality of a home service magazine, a touch of history, lots of how-to, and accurate information on traveling to historic sites and restorations. Each issue has a balance of the above elements. Articles can be on any subject but must be in the time period generally from 1700 to 1900. Length of articles should be from 1,000 to 3,000 words.

Articls must be illustrated. Submit color transparencies and drawings. Always give full credit on sources.

Payment varies and is upon acceptance. Query the Editor at *Early American Life*, Historical Times, Inc., 2245 Kohn Road, Box 8200, Harrisburg, Pennsylvania 7105.

Dolls and Dolls Collectors
DOLLMAKING

Dollmaking, The Magazine of Projects and Plans, is a quarterly publication for makers of dolls of every medium. The magazine includes projects for beginning, intermediate and advanced artists. The project can be explaining how a doll is made from start to finish; how a doll-related item or accessory such as a wig, shoes or complete costume is made; or a specific technique such as working with latex composition which can be used by a dollmaker in many projects. Most first articles are written on speculation. Length varies. Appropriate diagrams, patterns, b/w photos and/or color slides should be submitted with the article but there is no additional payment. Payment ranges from $100 to $200 and is made upon publication.

Sample copies are available for $2 each. Query the Editor at *Dollmaking*, Collector Communications Corp., 170 Fifth Avenue, New York, New York 10010.

DOLLS

Dolls, The Collector's Magazine is published bimonthly for doll collectors of antique, contemporary and reproduction dolls. It is a consumer magazine. Freelance articles of 500 to 2,000 words are needed and are done on speculation by first time writers. Subjects can be visits to outstanding public and private collections, problems of restoration, or a report on trends in doll collecting and investing. All submitted material must have a sharp collecting angle, including information on identification, availability and prices wherever pertinent and possible. Submit b/w glossy prints or color transparencies with the article. There is no additional payment for photos. Payment is up to $350.

Freelance material of up to 500 words and b/w photos are also used in the "Doll View" column. There is no byline given. Payment ranges from $25 to $75.

Dolls pays on publication and buys first North American serial rights. Query the Editor at *Dolls*, Collector Communications Corp., 170 Fifth Avenue, New York, New York 10010. Sample copies are available for $2 each.

MINIATURE COLLECTOR

Miniature Collector is a quarterly consumer magazine for collectors and makers of dollhouses, dollhouse furnishings and dolls and other miniatures. The magazine focuses on, but is not limited to, pieces in the scale of one inch equals one foot. Most first articles are written on speculation.

Ideas for articles include profiles and examination of the work of artisans involved in the making of miniatures; visits to outstanding public and private collections; profiles of well-known collectors and celebrities who collect miniatures; and material for the Projects & Plans Section which details do-it-yourself projects that can be accomplished easily in the average workshop. Diagrams, illustrations and/or b/w or color photos should accompany articles but there is no additional payment. Length ranges from 1,000 to 1,500 words. Payment is up to $200 and made upon publication. Usually buys first rights.

Sample copies are $1 each. Query the Editor at *Miniature Collector*, Collector Communications Corp., 170 Fifth Avenue, New York, New York 10010.

Handweaving
HANDWOVEN

Handwoven - Published five times a year: January, March, May, September and November by Interweave Press, Inc. which was established in 1975. *Handwoven* now has a circulation of 35,000. It addresses the interests of handweavers at all levels of mastery. Each issue includes handwoven designs to encourage the beginner and challenge the experienced weaver, full-color photography, complete instructions, yarn recommendations and suggested variations. Freelance articles of varying lengths are sought. They can range from book reviews and short pieces to in-depth features on technique, history and general weaving instruction.

Submit color transparencies and b/w glossy photos with your manuscript. Photos should be sharp, clear, have good contrast and a simple background. People in photos should be identified. If you submit swatches and samples, they should be no smaller than 4" x 4" and labeled. If you submit drawings and diagrams, they should be done in India ink (do not use felt-tipped pens) and ready for production. Lines must be sharp. If illustrations have labeled parts, please do this in light (non-reproductive) blue pen or pencil. *Handwoven* will re-do drafts to their specifications.

Payment is upon publication and starts at $15 and up for book reviews and other short pieces, and $50 to $100 for feature articles. Writers will receive a 50% non-use fee if an assigned manuscript is not published. Buys first North American serial rights.

Query the Editor at *Handwoven*, Interweave Press, 306 N. Washington Avenue, Loveland, Colorado 80537.

Jewelry Making
JEWELRY MAKING GEMS AND MINERALS

Jewelry Making Gems and Minerals, The Magazine That Shows You How is a monthly publication. It is how-to oriented. Readers want to know how to do it and where to find it. Two types of freelance articles are needed: how-to and field trip. Length varies. Photos should accompany articles. They can be 35 mm or larger transparencies (slides) or 3" x 4" or larger b/w prints.

Article payment is $.50 per column or $15 per page, including copy and photos. Color photos supplied by the author and used in the article are calculated at $1 per column inch.

Query the Editor at *Jewelry Making Gems and Minerals*, 555 Cajon Street, Suite B, Redlands, California 92373.

Leathercrafting
THE LEATHER CRAFTSMAN

The Leather Craftsman - Bimonthly dedicated to the preservation of leather craft and leather art. It has a readership of over 25,000. Each issue contains articles on prominent leather crafters, helpful hints and projects that *The Leather Craftsman* readers try at home or in their business. These projects of varying difficulty make the magazine a useful tool for the experienced craftsperson as well as the novice. All aspects of the craft including carving, stamping, dyeing, sewing, and decorating, are discussed by means of step-by-step instructions.

Articles can be any length. They should be written from the viewpoint of a leather craftsperson. The information should be specific enough so that readers can apply it to leathercrafting as easily as possible, depending upon their individual experience. Projects or articles should include good, clear photos or slides with a description of each. Send the project itself. The staff will then photograph it and return it to the writer. The project should also include a roughly drawn pattern (which will be redrawn by the staff artist if necessary) and step-by-step instructions. Directions should be simple and direct.

Payment is $50 to $200 for articles or projects and is made upon publication. Send finished articles or projects to *The Leather Craftsman*, P. O. Box 1386, Fort Worth, Texas 76101.

Machinist
THE HOME SHOP MACHINIST

The Home Shop Machinist, A Bimonthly Magazine Dedicated to Precision Metalworking - Readership ranges from novice to skilled machinist and engineer. In order to get an idea for the types of articles needed, read the magazine. Length varies. Buys all rights.

Photos and drawing will help to sell your article. B/w glossy prints and color prints that have good contrast and a clear image are sought. Drawings are also important but they must be perfect. Most authors will simply send sketches or blueprints of their drawings and the draftsperson will redraw them to size and line weight specifications.*The author is paid double the page rate for finished, inked drawings.* Reduce everything to 50%. Use the A.N.S.I. Drafting Standards as a guide. The standards can be obtained by writing to the American Society of Mechanical Engineers (ASME), United Engineering Center, 345 E. 47th Street, New York, New York 10017.

Payment is usually made upon acceptance. The rates are: $40, minimum per full published page; $9, published photos (each) with feature articles; $40, cover photo (rarely are cover photo submissions accepted that are unaccompanied by feature article material; $70, published pages with finished drawings (not requiring redrawing by the draftsperson); $30, short columns or articles less than full page; $15, filler items (less than half page); and $30, book reviews (already solicited).

Query the Editor at *The Home Shop Machinist,* P. O. Box 1810, Traverse City, Michigan 49685-1810.

Modeling
FINE SCALE MODELER (R)

Fine Scale Modeler(R), The Quality Modeling Magazine-Bimonthly which mostly stresses how-to-do-it techniques such as how to build a kit into a more accurate or more representative model; how to make parts you cannot buy, or parts that are better than what you can buy; how to paint a model, or a particular color scheme; or how to build a display or diorama. Nearly every aspect of modeling, including hints, tips, and workshop technique, can be considered a worthwhile subject for an article. Length can range from 750 to 3,000 words.

B/w prints and color transparencies (slides) should be submitted with the article. In addition, color photos should be "backed up" with a black-and-white negative or print, so that the magazine has the option of using either color or black-and-white, depending on where the article falls in the issue.

Payment is made upon acceptance. The minimum editorial rate is $30 per published page. The rate per page is increased when the author does a particularly good job, or when the material is especially timely or interesting. Articles that include camera-ready scale drawings also qualify for bonus rates.

Query the Editor at *Fine Scale Modeler*, A Kalmbach Publication, 1027 North Seventh Street, Milwaukee, Wisconsin 53233.

Needlepoint
NEEDLEPOINT NEWS

Needlepoint News - Bimonthly devoted exclusively to needlepoint. Published since 1974. The editors are looking for articles that educate and challenge the stitcher in terms of technique and new ideas.

Three types of freelance articles are needed: canvaswork techniques, project or how-to, and charted designs or patterns. **Canvaswork techniques** - step-by-step explanation of traditional or unconventional canvaswork. Timesavers, shortcuts, and unusual applications are possible approaches. Techniques to explore might be: types of stitches, applique, attachments, sculpting, shading, canvas painting, bargello, beading, pulled work or nue, needlelace, Rozashi, Teneriffe, working with various types of threads, stampwork methods, needleweaving over wire, petit point, and any of a host of other existing techniques. **Projects or how-to-articles-** *Needlepoint News* editors encourage the type of project that enables the stitcher to experiment with unusual techniques or designs. These can be any of the above techniques mentioned in canvaswork techniques incorporated into large or small projects (from rugs to miniatures). **Charted design or patterns** - For all designs, *Needlepoint News* requires a photo of the completed piece before accepting it for publication. Once accepted, the design is published in color and black-and-white, and a materials list is included with names of manufacturers or distributors of unusual or hard-to-find items needed for the design. Graphs or patterns need not be drawn letter-perfect; the art department will redraw them and provide the final touches.

Color slides (35 mm) or 3" x 4" (or larger) color prints should be submitted with the original designs or projects. Besides the color slides or prints, a graph, complete step-by-step instructions, a materials list, sources of supply and illustrations when necessary should be submitted.

Payment for original design articles is $75 per published page for First North American Serial Rights. If *Needlepoint News* chooses to purchase two-time publishing rights of a design or project for publication in the form of a book, booklet, pamphlet, brochure, manual, or anthology, payment will be $150 per published page. Payment for other articles is $35 per published page. Payment is made upon publication.

Query the Editor at *Needlepoint News*, E.G.W. Publishing Co., Box 5967, Concord, California 94524.

Pottery
AMERICAN CLAY EXCHANGE

American Clay Exchange, The Largest, Most Comprehensive Newsletter Devoted to American Made Pottery - Publication devoted exclusively to American made pottery, china, dinnerware (any clay items), the *American Clay Exchange (ACE)* is a twice-monthly (except July and December when it is published one time each). Freelance articles from small photographs on happenings in the pottery world to articles of 1,000 words are needed. The following information should be included in the article: dates pottery businesses opened and closed, marks on various pottery items, artists working at the companies and human interest information on the artists. *American Clay Exchange* normally buys all rights.

Photos will help to sell your article. B/w glossy photos are needed. They should contain only one or two items, should be shot up close to get the details of the items, and should be taken on a solid background. SX70 Polaroids are also acceptable.

There is also a possibility that writers who contribute articles frequently can become "contributing editors." Besides short and features articles, material is needed for the following columns: Roseville; Weller; Rookwood; book reviews on pottery, china, dinnerware or other clay subjects; specific pottery people in the news; titles; California potteries; dinnerware; novelties; and shows, exhibits, and flea markets.

Payment varies and is made upon acceptance. Query the Editor at the *American Clay Exchange*, 800 Murray Drive, El Cajon, California 92020.

Railroaders

LIVE STEAM

Live Steam, The Monthly Magazine for all Live Steamers and Large-Scale Railroaders Incorporating the Steam Power Quarterly Magazine - Read the magazine to obtain an idea for the type of articles needed. Many beginners read the magazine so it is necessary for the author to explain processes and techniques. Write the article like you are writing a letter to a friend.

Photos and drawings will help to sell your article. B/w glossy and color prints are the best. As far as drawings are concerned, most authors send in sketches or blueprints of their drawings and the draftsperson redraws them to the magazine's exacting style. If you can do finished drawings, the payment rate per page will double. Request the Draftsman's Guidelines from *Live Steam*. This sheet provides detail on styling, dimensional spacing, pen sizes, and lettering.

Payment rates are: $20, minimum per full published page; $6, published photos (each) with feature articles; $40, cover photo (*Live Steam* rarely accepts cover photo submissions that are unaccompanied by feature article material); $40, published pages with finished drawings (not requiring redrawing by the draftsman); $15, short columns or articles less than a full page; $10, filler items; and $20, book reviews. Payment is made quarterly following publication of the article.

Query the Editor at *Live Steam*, P. O. Box 629, Traverse City, Michigan 49684.

Woodworking
POPULAR WOODWORKING

Popular Woodworking - Bimonthly published since 1981. Its focus is on the interests of the modest production woodworker, small shop owner, wood craftsperson, advanced hobbyist, and woodcarver. Articles should address problems and solutions in production, marketing, design, or woodcraft techniques.

Eight types of freelance articles are sought: project with plans, techniques, jig journal, shop tip, marketing, musical instruments, living with Murphy, and out of the woodwork. **Projects with Plans (up to 1,500 words)** - Describe in clear, step-by-step format a project you think others would enjoy making. Include a cutting list and necessary diagrams. (Drawings need not be perfect; the *Popular Woodworking* staff can redraw them.) What woods, tools, techniques, and finishes did you use? Can the reader, by following your instructions, complete the project successfully? **Techniques (up to 1,500 words)** - Articles that explain special techniques used in woodworking such as how to cut certain joints and methods of work. Describe what the technique is applied for and why, and discuss tools used. If possible, include photos that show the process. **Jig Journal (up to 1,000 words)** - Discuss special set-ups and fixtures that help a tool do a particular task with ease. Include diagrams if appropriate. **Shop Tip (up to 300 words)** - Share with woodwork enthusiasts your special hint that has helped you so much. **Marketing (up to 1,500 words)** - Do you have a special marketing secret or experience that will assist others in selling their woodworking projects? Discuss successes, failures and what can be learned. **Musical Instruments (up to 1,500 words)** - Tell how to building a musical instrument from wood. Give a brief history of the instrument. Include what woods, tools, techniques and finishes are used. **Living with Murphy (up to 400 words)**- Murphy's Law: "If anything can go wrong, it will." And that certainly is the case with woodworking. How have you corrected woodworking errors? What are you careful to do now? What have you learned? **Out of the Woodwork (up to 150 words for humor; up to 400 words for other)** - Humorous and/or thought-provoking anecdotes or incidents that illustrate the wonderful world of woodworking.

B/w glossy photos (5" x 7" or larger). Include vertical as well as horizontal shots. Action and completed projects should be shown in photos. In some cases, color photography may be suitable. These should be 35 mm slides. These are in addition to the b/w photos. An extra $25 to $50 will be paid if a slide is chosen for the front cover.

Projects with plans, techniques and jig journal articles will receive $75 per published page for First North American serial rights. In some cases, two-time rights are bought at double the rate (or $150 per published page). For other articles, the rate is $45 per published page. Payment is upon publication.

Query the Editor at *Popular Woodworking*, 1300 Galaxy Way, Concord, California 94520.

WORKBENCH (R)

Workbench (R), the Do-It-Yourself Magazine - Bimonthly do-it-yourself woodworking, home improvement and home maintenance publication, published by Modern Handcraft, Inc. Freelance articles are needed on woodworking projects ranging from simple toys and other easy projects for the beginning woodworker to copies of museum furniture pieces for the expert craftsperson. Currently there is a need for articles on contemporary, practical home furnishings that would appeal to the woodworker with average skills. Also do-it-yourself articles are wanted that show how average people are using ingenuity to modernize their homes, improve their lifestyle and to reduce energy consumption. *Workbench* is also looking for articles that provide facts on reliable, inexpensive energy alternatives. Show the readers how they can incorporate these changes in their homes. Stories are also needed on maintenance and improvement of manufactured housing, including mobile homes. These stories should be detailed enough so readers can duplicate the project, possibly with modifications to suit their own needs or situations.

Article length varies.

With articles, submit detailed drawings of projects that are complete and accurately dimensioned. Pencil is acceptable. Include step-by-step instructions, facts, and a materials list, if appropriate. Blueprints are not required as all artwork is redrawn to fit a particular space. B/w glossy photos, 4" x 5" or larger should be included with the article. Color transparencies, 2-1/4" x 2-1/4" or larger are desired, but sharp 35 mm slides will be considered. *No instant color prints (Kodak or Polaroid)*. Additional payment is made for color photography.

Payment is usually $125 per published page and made upon acceptance. Query the Editor at **Workbench**, Modern Handcraft, Inc., 4251 Pennsylvania Avenue, Kansas City, Missouri 64111.

CHAPTER XX

RELIGIOUS MARKETS

Religious markets need material but as a rule they do not pay very well. Editors are looking for two types of material :1) personal experience writing that is relevant to the times and written for a wide audience; and 2) educational and inspiration material of interest to church members, workers and leaders within a denomination or religion. You do not have to be of the same faith as the publication you are submitting material to. For instance, I am a Catholic and I wrote an article titled, "Puppets' Messenger 'Bring God Closer.'" It appeared in *The Lutheran* magazine some years ago.

The verbatim text is as follows:

CITRUS SPRINGS, FLA--Sunday school enrollment has surged at this retirement community's Hope Evangelical Lutheran Church. Hope is the church where Pastor John L. Fox uses puppets to teach during church services.

Eighteen youngsters were attending Sunday School when Fox arrived at Hope eight months ago. The number today is 60. And adult membership has risen from 150 to more than 200.

Fox chose puppets after observing how much his two-year-old son learned by watching the show "Sesame Street". Eight cloth, button and yarn figures of animals are used by the 33-year-old minister. Fox's wife, Lynda, designed and made most of the puppets.

"The kids," he explains, "come to Sunday School and stay for church; some of them even without their parents.

The puppet shows break up the service for them, and they feel that they can get involved in the worship service and that at least some part of the worship speaks to them."

The show, he adds, "brings joy to many adults because of the expressions on the children's faces. Many unchurched people, I believe, have come to our church because the puppets speak to them in a simple theme. They don't get lost in theological jargon and long sermons."

In Fox's view, "Anyone can become a puppeteer. Just a little love, imagination, some creativity, and you can create laughter, joy, effective learning and bring God a little closer to those who are young at heart."

Hope Church, he says, "was built with the intention that there would be a small Sunday School. Already we are talking about additional educational rooms."

--Ruth Wucherer

How did I go about developing this article? First, I had a lead about Pastor Fox from *The Milwaukee Journal* newspaper. I queried *The Lutheran* magazine and the editor said he/she was interested in the idea. Second, I decided to call Pastor Fox over the phone and he gave me an interview. With the dateline, it looks like I went to Citrus Springs, Florida, but I did not. I used quite a few quotes in the article which I feel makes it quite readable. I also like that I received a byline. This was the first time I wrote for this publication. The article had a photo of Pastor Fox with two puppets.

What Types of Articles Does *The Lutheran* Need?

At present, *The Lutheran* is about 50% freelance written. It is a general interest magazine of the Lutheran Church in America and published twice a month except for the months of July, August and December, when it is published once a month. The editor is looking for articles for four main fields: Christian ideology; personal religious life, social responsibilities; Church as work; and human interest stories about people in whom considerable numbers of other people are likely to be interested. Every article should be based on a reasonable amount of research or should explore some source of information not readily available. Length of articles should be 500 to 2,000 words and payment is from $90 to $270. Articles are accepted on speculation. Buys one-time rights. Pays upon acceptance. Free sample copy and writer's guidelines. Query the Editor at *The Lutheran*, 2900 Queen Lane, Philadelphia, Pennsylvania 19129. Buys photos submitted with articles. Good 8" x 10" b/w glossy prints, pays $15 to $25. Color photos needed for the cover, pays up to $150.

In addition to *The Lutheran*, I recommend that you submit articles to the following ten publications. They are divided according to Catholic, Methodist, and Christian and interdenominational publications. Then they are arranged alphabetically.

Catholic Markets
CATHOLIC TWIN CIRCLE

Catholic Twin Circle is a national weekly Catholic newspaper which is distributed to Catholic churches as well as to individual subscribers around the country. A variety of articles are needed: inspirational stories (saints lives, and other true stories with a religious moral); interviews with Catholic personalities in the news; how-to advice on having a happy marriage or raising children today; and examinations of controversial issues affecting Catholics today. Articles range in length from 800 to 2,000 words. Payment is $.10 per published word. Photographs are accepted with the article but publication is not guaranteed. Query or submit complete article to Editor, *Catholic Twin Circle*, 6404 Wilshire Blvd., Suite 900, Los Angeles, California 90048.

COLUMBIA

Columbia is published monthly by the Knights of Columbus and has a circulation of 1,380,000. It is geared to a general Catholic audience but caters particularly to members of the Knights of Columbus and their families.

Fact articles of 2,500 to 3,500 words are sought. They should focus on some unique initiative of a local or state council of the Knights of Columbus. They can also deal with topics of interest to the Catholic layman and family such as current events, social problems, Catholic apostolic activities, programs and movements, rearing a family, and ecumenism, to name just a few. These articles must include substantial quotes from a variety of sources, particularly the recipients of any beneficent initiative. Twenty or more glossy color photos, transparencies or negatives with contact prints are required for illustration. Payment ranges from $600 to $750, including photos.

Buys all rights. Query the Editor at *Columbia*, P. O. Drawer 1670, New Haven, Connecticut 06507.

LIGUORIAN

Liguorian - A Catholic monthly magazine with a circulation of 570,000. Buys all rights but will reassign rights to author after publication upon request. According the writer's guidelines, *Liguorian's* purpose is to "lead our readers to a fuller Christian life by helping them to better understand the teachings of the gospel and the church and by illustrating how these teachings apply to life and the problems confronting them as members of families, the church, and society." Submit complete manuscript.

Articles should not exceed 2,000 words. Style and vocabulary should be readable. Use an interest-grabbing opening, state why the subject is important to readers, use examples, quotes, anecdotes, make practical applications, and end strongly. Manuscripts should be typewritten, double spaced and should include your name, address and *social security number.* Address manuscript to Editor, *Liguorian*, Liguori, Missouri 63057. *Liguorian* pays $.07 to $.10 a published word on acceptance.

ST. ANTHONY MESSENGER

St. Anthony Messenger is published monthly by the Franciscan Fathers of St. John the Baptist Province. It is a general-interest, family-oriented Catholic magazine. It is written and edited for people living in families on the family-like situations of church and community. The writer's guidelines say, "We want to help our readers better understand the teachings of the gospel and Catholic Church, and how they apply to life and the full range of problems confronting us as members of families, the church and society."

Nonfiction articles are needed for the following six categories: Church and religion; marriage, family and parenting; social; inspiration and practical spirituality; psychology; and profiles. Query first. State subject, sources, authorities and your qualifications to do the proposed article. Firsthand sources and authorities in the field should be consulted and interviewed. Articles should not exceed 3,000 words. Manuscripts should contain your name, address and social security number. Payment is $.12 a published word upon acceptance. Additional payment for photos if they are used.

A helpful "Information Sheet for Freelance Writers" with some recent articles in *St. Anthony Messenger* is available from the Editor at 1615 Republic Street, Cincinnati, Ohio 45210.

Methodist Publications

MATURE YEARS

Mature Years is the official publication for the United Methodist Church, prepared by the Board of Discipleship through the Curriculum Resources Committee and published quarterly by The Graded Press, 201 Eighth Avenue, South, P. O. Box 801, Nashville, Tennessee 37202. Articles of 1,200 to 1,500 words in length, dealing with all aspects of pre-retirement and retirement living are needed. Each issue is developed on a specific theme. Payment is usually $.04 a word.

Query at the address above. *Mature Years* prefers to purchase all rights. The Editor is especially interested in receiving short items (70 to 250 words) for a new department, "Ways to Expand One's Interests." Some special need or interest of general appeal to older adults is addressed. An example is tips on legal help. Submit the completed article.

Christian and Interdenominational Publications

AGLOW

Aglow, Today's Publication for Christian Women published bimonthly has a circulation of 75,000. *Aglow* editors are looking for 1,000 to 2,000 word articles written for women of all ages. The articles can take the form of the personal experience article, the personality article, the inspirational article, the how-to, the interview, or a scriptural teaching about Jesus Christ and his relationship to women today. The magazine uses personal photographs of the author and/or people involved in the article. Color snapshots are best. Payment for articles varies. Query first. Write Publications Department, Women's Aglow Fellowship International, P. O.

Box I, Lynnwood, Washington 98046-1556.

CHARISMA
Charisma, The Magazine About Spirit-led Living, is a monthly magazine covering Christianity -- especially the pentecostal/charismatic movement.

Very few articles are accepted from freelancers except those on assignment. All articles must be Christ-centered and helpful to the reader.

Several types of articles are wanted: personal teaching, college, issue, articles dealing with Israel, personal narrative, personality pieces, music and miracle story. Length usually ranges from 1,500 to 3,000 words.

Buys all rights. Pays $100 to $150 first-time authors, more for those who have written for the magazine.

Authors should submit a manuscript if they have not been published in *Charisma* and a query if they have already been published. The address of *Charisma* is 190 N. Westmonte Drive, Altamonte Springs, Florida 32714.

CHRISTIAN LIFE
Christian Life, The Magazine of Spiritual Renewal, is a monthly read by leadership groups in evangelical Christian circles.

Types of articles sought: trend, inspirational, adventure, personality profiles, people on the move profiles, general features, devotional, and all in a woman's day "shorties". Length varies.

Payment is $50 for short articles and up to $250 to $300 for full-length articles. Color or b/w photos may be submitted but there is no additional payment: 35 mm, 2-1/4" x 2-1/4" or 4" x 5" transparencies or color prints, or 5" x 7" or 8" x 10" glossy b/w prints.

Buys all rights. Query the Editor at *Christian Life*, 396 E. St. Charles Road, Wheaton, Illinois 60188.

THE OTHER SIDE
The Other Side is published every five weeks (every six weeks during January and July). It has a paid circulation of about 14,000 and is published by Jubilee, an independent Christian organization committed to justice rooted in discipleship. According to the "Guidelines for Writers," *The Other Side* aims to be personal, practical and joyful. It tries

to help its readers see 'the other side' of American affluence -- the world of the poor, the oppressed, and the exploited, both here and abroad. While it seeks to put its readers in touch with the oppression, injustice, and militarism of our world, it also seeks to put them in touch with the hope and joy of knowing that God is at work and that God's people are responding to faithfulness to the biblical version. The magazine addresses a wide range of social, economical, political, and spiritual issues from a radical Christian perspective. It aims to encourage and stimulate readers in the lifestyle of discipleship.

Readers of this publication come from a wide variety of Christian traditions -- evangelicals, mainline Protestants, Charismatic, Episcopalians, Roman Catholics, Quakers, Mennonites and others. What they have in common is a commitment to applying the teachings of Christ to contemporary life. They are activists who care deeply about the biblical vision of shalom.

Freelance submissions are accepted in the following departments: "Discoveries," "Partners," "Simple Pleasures," "Parenting," "Bread for the Journey," and "Editors' Choice."

"Discoveries" - In each issue, the editors feature three to five short profiles of interesting people, unusual groups, surprising churches, or innovative local efforts. The subject of each profile should be relatively new to most readers, not an individual or group with a national reputation or following. Each article should have lots of personal quotes and vivid description. Length runs between 500 and 1,100 words. Photos are a must.

"Partners" - Features one or two people centered profiles of nationally established groups that work for peace or justice from a Christian framework. These profiles must reveal, in a brief way, something of the character of these groups -- what readers would be interested to discover for themselves if they were able to drop in on the group's operations for a day, including some description of what the people who work there are like, what motivates them, how they feel about their successes and failures, what the office environment is like, and what the mood of the organization is -- plus something of the group's future dreams and plans. Each article should conclude with a brief note listing the name, address, and phone number of the organization. Length can be from 700 to 1,500 words, but shorter lengths are preferred. Photos are a must.

"Simple Pleasures" - This department explores the joys of simple and alternative lifestyles through short how-to pieces, idea articles, personal experiences, profiles of people who are living in fun and innovative ways, or personal essays in which the author wrestles with significant simple-living questions. Length should run from 300 to 1,500 words. Photos are preferred.

The department, **"Parenting"** needs articles that provide practical help and encouragement to parents who care about peace, justice, and Christian faith. Articles should especially emphasize parents who feel bewildered and alone. Length should be between 500 and 1,800 words.

"Bread for the Journey" needs features that tell about study and retreat centers where the reader can go. First person writing is preferred and the article should make readers feel they have just experienced the place firsthand. At the end of the article, the writer should indicate the center's name, address, and phone number -- with additional information on who to contact for reservations, fees, and housing arrangements. Length should be between 500 and 1,000 words. Photos are a must.

"Editors' Choice" - Contains short, capsule-style reviews of worthwhile books, records and films. Books should appeal to a majority of readers, not just academics. Reviews should be between 175 and 400 words. They should be short, tightly written, and personal in character, specific rather than general. Introductory notes to book reviews should include title, author, publisher, number of pages, year published, and current price of the cheapest edition. Introductory notes to record reviews should include title, performer, record distributor, year produced, and standard retail price of the recording. Introductory notes to movie reviews should include title of movie, name of the director, name of the producer, name of the distributor, and year produced. Because of the magazine's publication schedule, movie reviews should be submitted as soon as possible after the movie's first introductory showings so that the review can appear in *The Other Side* while the film is in mass distribution.

Payment for feature articles usually ranges from $25 to $200. Payment for reviews is from $10 to $20. Payment for material used in the magazine's other departments ranges from $25 to $100.

The Other Side prefers to purchase all rights to a manuscript. When an author's article is accepted, he or she will be sent a written publication agreement. Queries are preferred but not necessary. They can be either done by phone or mail. To query, telephone 703-371-7416 or 215-849-2178; or write the Editor at *The Other Side*, Box 3948, Fredericksburg, Virginia 22402. Even though the magazine is published in Pennsylvania, queries should be addressed to the Virginia office.

SUNDAY DIGEST

Sunday Digest is a weekly, nondenominational, adult take-home paper. These types of articles are needed: personal experience (first-person narratives), how-to articles that have a spiritual emphasis, lighthearted articles, and one-page anecdotes. Length ranges from 500 to 1,500 words.

Buys First North American Serial Rights. Pays a minimum of $.07 per word.

Queries are not necessary. The address is Editor, *Sunday Digest*, 850 North Grove Avenue, Elgin, Illinois 60120.

CHAPTER XXI

JUVENILE, TEEN AND YOUNG ADULT PUBLICATIONS

Juvenile, teen and young adult publications are avenues for freelance writers to sell their writings. On the whole, these markets are not high paying. Still, some writers would like to submit their works to these markets.

The juvenile publications are for three age groups: two to five year olds, six to eight year olds, and nine to twelve year olds. Sometimes the publications overlap on ages. Teen and young adult publications cover the years 12 to 18.

I have divided the publications into two categories, juvenile, and teen and young adult and then have arranged them alphabetically. There are 13 moneymaking opportunities in all! *Ranger Rick* is an excellent paying market so I recommend that you check out the types of articles the editor wants.

Juvenile Publications

CLUBHOUSE

Clubhouse - Published ten times a year and copyrighted by Your Story Hour. This is a Christian magazine for children between the ages of 9 and 13. Its primary goal is to let children who have little or no Christian influence in their lives know there is a God and that He loves kids, but it is not religiously oriented in an overt way. The magazine is designed to help young people feel good about themselves.

Writers can submit several types of freelance articles: stories which demonstrate honesty, selflessness and bravery in action; stories in which children or adults are heroic, wise and kind; articles which are exciting, full of adventure, true or true-to-life, upbeat, dramatic and dynamic; historical articles; stories which portray the problems encountered by the use of drug, alcohol and tobacco; articles related to parent-child or boy-girl relationships; and parables.

Three article formats are used. The first is lead articles of 1,000 to 1,200 words. The second is "Story Cukes" of 600 to 800 words which can be broken into 4 to 6 sections, each of which will have its own illustration in *Clubhouse's* checkerboard layout. The third format is "Thinker Tales" which are parables of 600 to 800 words written in classic or modern styles that teach Christian principles on relevant topics.

Payment is $35 for lead articles, $30 for "Story Cukes" and "Thinker Tales."

Query the Editor at *Clubhouse*, Box 15, Berrien Springs, Michigan 49103.

COBBLESTONE (R)

Cobblestone (R), The history Magazine for Young People- Monthly American history magazine for young people ages 8 to 14. Each issue has a specific theme. Writers should request the "Writers' Guidelines and Theme List" so they will know the topics ahead of time. This list also contains query deadlines. Historical accuracy and live, original approaches to subjects are the primary concerns of the editors in choosing materials.

Three types of freelance articles are needed: features, supplemental nonfiction and activities. **Feature Articles** - Nonfiction, plays and biographies of 800 to 1,200 words. Pay $.13 to $.15 per printed word. **Supplemental Nonfiction**- Includes subjects directly and indirectly related to the theme. Editors like little-known information but encourage writers not to overlook the obvious. Length of 200 to 800 words. Payment of $.10 to $.12 per printed word. **Activities** - Crafts, recipes, and woodworking projects that can be done either by children alone or with adult supervision. Length up to 1,000 words. Query should be accompanied by sketches and description of how the activity relates to the theme. Payment for these materials is made on an individual basis.

Cobblestone purchases all rights to materials. A sample issue is available for $3.95. Query the Editor-in-Chief at *Cobblestone*, Cobblestone Publishing, Inc., 20 Grove Street, Peterborough, New Hampshire 03458.

THE FRIEND

The Friend - Monthly published by The Church of Jesus Christ of Latter-Day Saints for boys and girls up to twelve years of age. The magazine is circulated worldwide.

Some of the types of freelance articles needed are those that focus on character-building qualities without moralizing or preaching, children resolving conflict, holiday, sports, humor, and manuscripts that portray various cultures. These articles should be no longer than 1,000 words. Short articles on various subjects are needed for young readers and preschool children. The length should be no longer than 250 words.

Payment is $.08 a word and up. *The Friend* does not pay for articles written by children. *The Friend* purchases all rights to manuscripts accepted.

Submit completed manuscript to the Editor at *The Friend*, 23rd Floor 50 E. North Temple, Salt Lake City, Utah 84150.

HAPPY TIMES

Happy Times, The Magazine That Builds Character and Confidence - Full color, non-denominational magazine published 10 times a year for children 3 to 10 years of age. One of the magazine's purposes is to teach positive character traits. Each issue has a theme and all material should reinforce that theme. The magazine is very specialized and the best way to get a feeling for what type of material is needed is to read back issues of the magazine. Free sample copies are available upon request for 5 stamps or $1.30 to cover postage. Subscription order blanks are also available.

Three types of freelance material are needed: bedtime stories, field trip articles and science articles. **Bedtime Stories** - These five page stories of 350 to 600 words appear in the back of each magazine. Each story features the life of a famous person. The more famous and recognizable the subject, the better the chance the story will be published in *Happy Times*. The subject featured in one of these bedtime stories is someone who strongly exemplifies the character trait featured in that issue. Examples: in an issue on caring,

Florence Nightingale was featured; in an issue on industry, Benjamin Franklin was featured. Payment is $30 to $100.
Field Trip Articles - These articles spotlight different professions such as policemen, nurses and dentists. Length should be no longer than 200 words. Payment is $10 to $50. If amateur Kodachrome slides are submitted by authors and are satisfactory, illustration rates will be paid when published.
Science Articles - These articles written by doctors, engineers, scientists or other professionals should accurately explain science concepts that are simple, exciting and understandable to children. Length should be no longer than 200 words. Payment is from $10 to $50.

Writers should request the "Happy Times Theme List" and "Bedtime Stories Already Published in Happy Times Magazine." These lists will give writers an idea of what has been published and what will be published. *Happy Times* purchases First North American serial rights. Payment is made upon publication.

Send queries to the Copy Editor at *Happy Times*, 5600 North University Avenue, Provo, Utah 84604 or completed manuscripts to the Managing Editor and Art Director at the same address.

POCKETS

Pockets - A devotional magazine for children which is published by The Upper Room. It is published monthly except January. The purpose of *Pockets* is to open up the fullness of the gospel of Jesus Christ to children. It is written and produced for children and designed to help children pray and be in relationship to God. The magazine emphasizes that children are loved by God and that God's grace calls them into community. It is through the community of God's people that children experience that love in their daily lives.

Pockets is for children six through twelve, with a target reading age of eight through eleven. Though some may share it with their families, it is designed primarily for the personal use of children.

Pockets accepts freelance nonfiction articles from adults and children. The articles should be related to a particular theme which has been projected. This list of themes and due dates is available from the editorial office. A stamped, self-addressed envelope should be provided. In addition, articles about the Bible, church history, the liturgical year, various holidays and cultures are wanted. *Pockets* also seeks biographical sketches of persons, famous or unknown, whose lives reflect their Christian commitments and values. These may be either short vignettes (a single incident) or longer and more complete biographies. Length of articles should be 400 to 600 words.

Pockets purchase first periodical rights. Payment is $.07 and up a word. An honorarium will be paid for a manuscript that needs little or no editing. Payment is made at the time the article is purchased.

Mail complete manuscripts to the Editor at *Pockets*, 1908 Grand Avenue, Box 189, Nashville, Tennessee 37202-0189.

R-A-D-A-R

R-A-D-A-R - Quarterly published in weekly parts, *R-A-D-A-R* is a take-home paper for boys and girls who are in grades 3 to 6. Its goal is to reach children with the truth of God's Word, and to help them make it the guide of their lives. Many of *R-A-D-A-R's* features, including its stories, now correlate with the Sunday School lesson themes. Writers should send for a quarterly theme list and sample copies of *R-A-D-A-R*.

Freelance articles of 400 to 500 words are needed on hobbies, animals, nature, life in other lands, sports, science, and seasonal subjects to name just a few. Articles should have a religious emphasis and should be documented with sources that have been used. Payment is up to $.02 a word. Additional payment is made for photos.

Query the Editor at *R-A-D-A-R*, Standard Publishing, 8121 Hamilton Avenue, Cincinnati, Ohio 45231.

RANGER RICK

Ranger Rick - Monthly publication of the National Wildlife Federation (NWF), a nonprofit corporation. *Ranger Rick's* audience ranges in age from six to twelve, though the reading level of most materials is aimed at nine-year-olds or fourth graders. *It is an excellent paying market.*

Full-length feature articles of 900 words are wanted on any aspect of nature, outdoor adventure and discovery, pets, science, conservation or related subjects. To find out what subjects have been covered recently, writers should consult *Ranger Rick's* annual indexes. These are available in many libraries or are free upon request from *Ranger Rick's* editorial offices. All articles are accepted on speculation.

The National Wildlife Federation discourages the keeping of wildlife as pets so the keeping of pets should not be featured in articles. Human qualities may be attributed to animals only in fantasy stories, where it will be obvious to readers that you are not writing about real animals. List all references when submitting the finished work, unless you are an expert in the field. It is strongly recommended that a writer consult with experts in the field when developing material and that one of them read the finished manuscript for accuracy before it is submitted to *Ranger Rick*.

Payment ranges up to $350 depending on quality. Upon acceptance of an article, a transfer of rights form will be sent to the writer. The National Wildlife Federation prefers to buy all world rights. Payment will be processed after *Ranger Rick's* staff receives the signed transfer of rights form.

Query the Editors at *Ranger Rick*, 1412 16th Street, N.W., Washington, D.C. 20036-2266.

WEE WISDOM (R)

Wee Wisdom (R), A Children's Magazine from Unity-Published monthly, except bimonthly in June/July and August/September by United School of Christianity. Its purpose is to help children develop character and their full potential. Character-building ideals should be emphasized without preaching. Language should be universal, avoiding the Sunday School image. Prospective writers should request several sample copies so that they will be able to study the style.

Short, lively nature and science stories, puzzles and projects, and simple handcraft projects are sought. Stories and articles should range in length from 500 to 800 words, and although entertaining enough to hold the interest of older children, they should be readable by a third-grader.

Payment for articles is at a minimum of three cents a word and up. Payment is made upon acceptance. Unity School buys first publication rights which include the right to serialize the work and the right to edit every work to assure conformance with Unity School of Christianity's literary and artistic standards. All material is copyrighted in the name of Unity School, and Unity School asks for permission to republish the work in future publications at its discretion.

Send query to the Editor at *Wee Wisdom*, Unity School of

Christianity, Unity Village, Missouri 64065.

Teen and Young Adult Publications

GROUP

Group (R), The Young Ministry Publisher - Group is the interdenominational magazine for leaders of high-school-age Christian youth groups. Its purpose is to supply ideas and inspiration. It is published eight times a year. In *Group*, there is an insert called Group Members Only whose purpose is to help young people grow in their faith. It is also published eight times a year.

Articles are needed for four area: Group, Group Members Only, "Try This One" and "News, Trends and Tips." **Group**-Need articles that tell about successful youth groups or youth group projects. Groups involved in music, drama, art, helping others, and missionary work are regularly featured. Length of 1,200 to 1,700 words. Payment of up to $150. **Group Members Only** - Wanted are articles written to senior young people. Articles should not preach or speak down to teenagers. How-to articles on improving self-image and relationships with family and friends are welcomed. Articles are also sought on strengthening faith and seeing how it applies in everyday life. Length of 800 to 1,000 words. Payment of up to $150. **"Try This One" Section** - Short ideas for group use are needed. These include games, crowd breakers, discussion starters, role plays, worship ideas and fund raisers. Length of up to 300 words. Payment is $15. **"News, Trends and Tips" section** - Articles are sought on brief leadership tips such as how to lead effective discussions and how to increase enthusiasm. Length of up to 500 words. Payment is $25. All payment is made upon acceptance of articles.

Query the Editor at *Group*, Thom Schultz Publications, Inc., 425 E. Eisenhower Blvd., P. O. Box 481, Loveland, Colorado 80539.

GUIDE

Guide is a weekly, Seventh-day Adventist journal geared for 10 to 15 year olds. Stories should be presented from the viewpoint of a young teenager, be true and include dialogue.

Positive aspects of Christian living -- faithfulness, obedience to parents, perseverance, kindness and courtesy -- should be stressed in the stories. Stories are especially needed about boys, school experiences, and ethnic groups from their own perspective. Some animal stories, and a few articles on nature and outdoor activities are also bought. Length ranges from 1,000 to 2,500 words.

Guide pays upon acceptance, $.02 to $.04 per word, and buys first serial rights.

Query first. The address is *Guide*, Office of the Editor, 55 W. Oak Ridge Drive, Hagerstown, Maryland 21740.

SEVENTEEN MAGAZINE

Seventeen Magazine - Monthly which accepts articles on subjects of interest to teenagers. Writers are advised to go through a year's worth of back issues (most libraries carry the publication) to learn more about what the magazine publishes. Desired length varies from 800 words for short features and monthly columns to 2,500 words for major articles.

Seventeen gives assignments (guarantees a few) only to writers who have been published in the magazine or whose professional work is known to the editors. Thus, writers whose work has not appeared in *Seventeen* should include a list of his or her writing credits and tear sheets of published articles. Writers who have had no articles, or only a few published, will be asked to write on speculation which means payment is not guaranteed.

Payment varies depending on the piece's placement in the magazine, quality and length. It is made upon acceptance. Extra payment is made for photographs or artwork. These are paid for after they are scheduled for a particular issue.

Send queries or manuscripts to the Senior Editor or the Articles Editor at *Seventeen* Magazine, 850 Third Avenue, New York, New York 10022.

STRAIGHT

Straight is a weekly magazine for Christian teenagers, published quarterly by the Standard Publishing Company. These types of articles are needed: devotional, current issues from a Christian point of view, and humor. Topics that are covered include school, family life, recreation, friends, part-time jobs, dating and music. Length varies. B/w glossy photos may be submitted with articles.

Payment is made upon acceptance. *Straight* pays $.02 per word for first rights, and $.01 to $.015 per word for reprint rights. Photos bring $15 to $25 for first use, and $10 to $15 for reuse.

Query the Editor, *Straight*, 8121 Hamilton Avenue, Cincinnati, Ohio 45231.

YOUNG AND ALIVE

Young and Alive is a monthly magazine for blind and visually impaired young adults between the ages of 16 and 20. It is published in braille and large print for an interdenominational Christian audience.

Feature material is sought: adventure, biography, camping, health, history, hobbies, nature, practical Christianity, sports and travel. Also needed are nonfiction stories (such as serials, parables, satire), devotional/inspirational articles and informative articles. Length should be 800 to 1,400 words. *Young and Alive* pays $.03 to $.05 a word upon acceptance.

Photos should accompany the manuscript. They should be b/w glossy prints. Payment is $3 to $4 for each photo upon acceptance.

Query the Editor at *Young and Alive*, 4444 South 52 Street, Lincoln, Nebraska 68516.

CHAPTER XXII

GARDEN AND HOME PUBLICATIONS

Closely allied to hobby and craft publications are garden and home magazines. Many people like to have a lovely garden. You are probably dying to share your secrets about your successful garden with readers. Here's your chance!

I have arranged the publications alphabetically. Some cover all areas of the United States while others are regional. They also cover topics other than gardens and homes.

BETTER HOMES AND GARDENS

Better Homes and Gardens is a monthly magazine. Articles are needed for the following areas: travel, education, health, cars, money management and home entertainment. Length varies. Read several issues to become familiar with the style of the magazine.

The magazine buys all rights and pays upon acceptance. The payment rate is based on estimated length, quality, and importance of the published article.

Query first. The address of *Better Homes and Gardens* is Locust at 17th, Des Moines, Iowa 50336.

GARDEN DESIGN

Garden Design - Monthly which features the gardens of others. Freelance articles are needed which describe elements that make the garden special: intent, design, solutions to unique problems, features, topography, seasonal qualities, plant materials and their uses, furnishings and garden ornaments. When writing the article, use a conversational tone. Describe the garden as it is and tell how it came to be. Also credit landscape architects, designers, architects, interior designers, consultants or the garden owners (if permission has been granted). In the article, include a plan of the location. Include boundaries, compass orientation, pertinent site features and major structures (with exterior doors and windows if important). The average article runs between four and six double-spaced typewritten pages.

Payment rates are as follows: feature text, $300; department text, $200; and department contribution, $50. If the submitted article requires substantial rewriting, *Garden Design* will pay a $100 research fee for the information supplied. The kill fee for an assigned accepted article is $100.

Query the Editor at *Garden Design*, 1733 Connecticut Avenue, N.W., Washington, D.C. 20009.

GURNEY'S GARDENING NEWS

Gurney's Gardening News - Bimonthly tabloid newspaper is published by Gurney Seed and Nursery Corporation. It is a 119-year-old company which offers home gardeners more than 4,000 items -- seeds, ornamentals, gardening and kitchen aids in spring and fall catalogs. More than half of *Gurney's Gardening News* readers work large gardens (40x50 feet), have gardened for 20 or more years and live in small town or rural areas. They know gardening! The publication welcomes articles which give all gardening viewpoints and philosophies from organic to chemical. The purpose of the newspaper is to promote gardening and, therefore, the editors like articles to inform, stimulate and invite readers to experiment with new varieties and try different gardening techniques.

Three types of freelance articles are needed: how-to, general interest, and food articles and recipes. **How-to** articles should include information on plant culture. Points to be considered include temperature, sun, soil drainage, and fertilization. Plant descriptions should be very specific and include information on height, width, color, flower size, and rate of growth. **General interest** articles cover gardener profiles, unusual gardens, unusual techniques, and innovations in food preservation. In the gardener profile articles, include unusual and unique ideas or methods that have proved successful for the gardener and may be adopted by others.

Food articles and recipes - Use figures for all references, in ingredients and instructions, unless it is necessary to spell out a word to avoid confusion; e.g., "two 5-inch squares." The preferred length for articles averages 1,000 words. Articles are bought on speculation.

Payment for articles is $.10 per word and made upon acceptance. Buys first North American serial rights.

Additional payment for photos is made. It ranges from $10 to $20 per photo. B/w photos (5" x 7" or 8" x 10" size) are needed.

Query the Editor at *Gurney's Gardening News*, 2nd and Capitol, Yankton, South Dakota 57079.

HOME MECHANIX

Home Mechanix is a monthly magazine which stresses how to manage your house and auto better. Freelance writers can break in most easily by submitting articles on home improvement and workshop or consumer products and services. For home improvement and workshop articles, a writer should tell about one project he or she has done to improve the home. It should be a how-to story giving step-by-step instructions for building. Such information as time and cost and materials used should be included in the article. All how-to articles must be well illustrated with photos and drawings. Consumer products and services articles cover such subjects as gardening, satellite TV, energy, home entertainment systems, boating, buying guides, bicycles, design and hobbies, to name just a few.

With each article, photos should be submitted: 8" x 10" glossy b/w prints, 2-1/4" x 2-1/4" or 35 mm color transparencies. There is no separate payment for photos.

Payment varies from $300 to $500 per published page depending on how much work the editor has to do to make the article publishable. *Home Mechanix* buys all rights and pays upon acceptance.

Query the specific editor: general features, home improvement and workshop or consumer products. The address of *Home Mechanix* is 1515 Broadway, New York, New York 10036.

NATIONAL GARDENING

National Gardening - Monthly publication of the non-profit National Gardening Association. The magazine combines "how-to" gardening information with general articles of interest to home and community gardeners: unusual gardens, gardeners, plants, methods and systems, innovations in food preservation, nutritional knowledge, soil science, environmental issues relevant to gardeners, self-sufficiency and homesteading with the accent on gardens. Authors should primarily focus on food growing. A conversational writing style touched with humor where appropriate is recommended.

Other subjects for freelance articles are gardens which have a special focus: therapy gardens for the handicapped, prison gardens, and community gardens of all sorts -- school, church, retirement and corporate. Additional subjects include news directly connected with food gardens and orchards: inventions and discoveries, natural happenings, new varieties, endangered species, and experienced gardeners' special techniques to improve any segment of the seed-to-harvest process.

Articles can range from 300 to 3,000 words. Payment is made upon acceptance and ranges from $40 to $250. Buys one-time use.

Photos will help to sell your article. These can be glossy b/w photos or Kodachrome 64 slides. Payment ranges from $10 to $40 and $100 minimum for cover shots for one-time use. Payment is made upon publication.

Query the Editor at *National Gardening*, National Gardening Association, 180 Flynn Avenue, Burlington, Vermont 05401.

RODALE'S ORGANIC GARDENING

Rodale's Organic Gardening - Organic Gardening, now *Rodale's Organic Gardening*, was started in 1942 by J. I. Rodale, founder of Rodale Press. His original purpose was to present the advantages of using organic methods to produce better quality food. Very simply, this method is based on building the health and life of the soil with compost, organic materials such as grass clippings, leaves and other non-synthetic amendments such as manure, bonemeal, cottonseed meal, green sand and hand picking, or using barriers to control pests when necessary. Other important aspects include attracting beneficial insects which prey on pets, planting disease resistant varieties, and practicing rotation and interplanting to improve productivity.

What are some of the major subject areas *Rodale's Organic Gardening* covers? They are: vegetables; fruits and nuts; soil, compost and non-synthetic soil amendments; biological pest control; landscaping and design; perennial and annual flowers; bulbs; lawns; trees and shrubs; herbs; preparing and preserving fresh produce; garden tools and equipment; environmental issues; and profiles of breeders, and experienced gardeners. Articles can range from 800 to 4,800 words but 1,600 to 2,400 words is preferred. Articles are looked at on speculation.

Payment for articles is upon acceptance and ranges from $.20 to $.30 per word. Payment is based on varying factors such as amount of editing required, submission of photographs or help in finding them. If an article falls short of requirements, a kill fee of 20% is paid.

Photo payment is separate and varies. For b/w, negatives are preferred. *Rodale's Organic Gardening* staff can convert color to b/w, so if you are shooting, use color slide film (Ektachrome is best for shooting greenery). For color, transparencies should be sent.

Query the Editorial Director at *Rodale's Organic Gardening*, 33 East Minor Street, Emmaus, Pennsylvania 18049.

TEXAS GARDENER

Texas Gardener (R), The Magazine for Texas Gardeners, by Texas Gardeners - Bimonthly for a readership of over 30,000. Since growing conditions are so different in Texas, *Texas Gardener* readers want to know specific information on how to make gardening succeed in the Lone Star State. All articles must, therefore, reflect this slant. The magazine covers vegetable and fruit production, as well as ornamental and home landscaping information.

Two types of articles re needed: technical and feature. Technical articles should explain how to do some aspect of gardening (e.g., graft pecans, plant bulbs) in a clear, easy-to-follow manner, and must be accurate. All technical articles should refer to experts in the field. Accompanying photos and/or illustrations are essential. **Feature articles** can focus on interviews/profiles of Texas gardeners who are hobbyists or professional horticulturists and doing something unique, or on new gardening techniques. These are only a couple suggestions.

Article length can be from 8 to 12 double-spaced, typed pages but 4 to 6 typed pages is preferred. Pays $50 to $200 upon acceptance and buys all rights.

Photos help sell the article. High-quality color transparencies and clear b/w prints, either 5" x 7" or 8" x 10", and b/w contact sheets. Pay is negotiable. Buys all rights.

Articles are bought on speculation. Query first with clips of published works or a writing sample and a list of areas of expertise. The address is: Editor, **Texas Gardener**, P. O. Box 9005, Waco, Texas 76714-9005.

CHAPTER XXIII

NEWSPAPERS AND NEWSPAPER MAGAZINES

Another avenue for a beginning writer to have a freelance article published is in a daily or weekly newspaper. I suggest that you call or set up an appointment with an editor of a local newspaper. Perhaps he or she will let you submit material on speculation. If you submit work on a regular basis, you may even become a stringer. In many cases, you will get paid.

A few years ago, I took a trip to Washington, D.C. One of the sites I visited was Mount Vernon, George Washington's home. I discovered that Ann Pamela Cunningham and the Mount Vernon Ladies' Association were responsible for restoring the estate. I decided to write an article and it was published in *The Milwaukee Journal* newspaper, a daily newspaper. I reside in Milwaukee, Wisconsin.

So that readers can get a feel for newspaper style, I have provided the entire text verbatim. The article had one photo. At the time I wrote the article, I was paid for it and also received a byline. The article was dated February 10, 1974.

**THEY KEPT MOUNT VERNON FROM
CRUMBLING TO RUIN
ANN CUNNINGHAM AND HER FRIENDS RAISED
THE MONEY TO PRESERVE WASHINGTON'S ESTATE
By Ruth Wucherer,
Journal Special Correspondent**

The home of George Washington in Mount Vernon, Virginia, would not have been restored had it not been for Ann pamela Cunningham. She passed the decaying home in 1853 while on a steamboat going down the Potomac River. It had been a tradition for each craft equipped with a bell to toll it in passing Mount Vernon.

She was shocked by the sight. This led her to form the Mount Vernon Ladies' Association of the Union in 1853, the first official restoration group in the U.S., and the Women's Patriotic Society. Today, as then, the members serve without remuneration.

Raising $200,000 a Formidable Job

Raising the amount of $200,000 to buy Mount Vernon was a formidable task. On December 2, 1853, the 37 year old Mrs. Cunningham petitioned for money in a Southern newspaper; she first signed herself as "A Southern Matron" because women were only mentioned in the paper when they married or died. She later stated her real name.

In 1856, Mrs. Cunningham had the fortune of meeting a great orator, the Rev. Edward Everett, in Richmond. He was giving a lecture on George Washington. Mrs. Cunningham told him about her work and Everett decided to speak all over the country about restoring Mount Vernon.

He donated $69,024 of his earnings to the association. The remainder was raised by the states and through public subscription.

Mrs. Cunningham then approached John Augustine Washington, Jr., George Washington's great-grandnephew, about selling the estate. At first he did not answer, but in 1858 the Mount Vernon Ladies' Association bought the 200 acre tract, including the mansion, wharf and all subsidiary buildings for $200,000. Today there are nearly 500 acres.

Acquiring Mount Vernon was a great accomplishment for Mrs. Cunningham, who had an injured spine as a result of a fall from a horse at the age of 16. She was originally from South Carolina, was married and had a daughter, but sources do not state when and to whom she was married. In 1874, she resigned from the association.

Gave Souvenirs to Many Visitors

While the mansion itself remained, its furnishings had been distributed among the members of the Washington and Custis families or sold by executors after the death of Mrs. Washington in 1802. Mrs. Washington also had the habit of giving away small souvenirs such as spoons to visitors. This, in turn, made it hard for the association to acquire items, but today most of the pieces on the first floor and all those in the master's bedroom are original.

George Washington occupied Mount Vernon from 1759, when he married Martha Custis, a widow with two children, to 1775. He visited it periodically after 1775, but did not come back until 1797, when he retired. He died at Mount Vernon on December 14, 1799. Lund Washington, a distant cousin, managed the estate in his absence. Washington often left notes on what should be done.

The estate has the flavor of the plantation life of the 18th century. The placement of numerous gardens, trees and shrubs adds variation to what otherwise would be just a series of buildings. Washington himself loved plants and experimented with them in his botanical garden. The garden, today, has been replanted, but has many of the plants the original garden had.

Washington had a feel for design, even though architecture was not an established profession. The mansion is characterized by the elegant, high columned piazza, extending the full length of the house. The exterior finish of the mansion and its courtyard dependencies is unusual. The siding was beveled to give an appearance of stone; sand was applied to the freshly painted surface.

The mansion contains the banquet hall, central hall, little parlor, west parlor, dining room, bedrooms, kitchen pantry and library, which was Washington's headquarters. It is located on the north end. Here he wrote letters about the establishment of the federal government, received the reports of overseers, made daily entries in his dairy and posted his accounts.

In the little parlor is the harpsichord that belonged to Nelly Custis, Martha Washington's granddaughter. Washington especially loved her playing, because he could not play himself. The harpsichord is associated with his last happy public appearance. Charming Nelly was the apple of his eye, and her wedding to his nephew, Lawrence Lewis, was celebrated on his last birthday, February 22, 1979. He died in December.

Self-Sufficient Estate Once Employed 250

Mount Vernon has a villagelike character, with the mansion being the seat of government and the surrounding buildings its dependencies. Washington planned it this way so that the people who worked for him would not intrude upon him. Still, he would go around often and help them with their problems.

Since 250 people at one time worked at the mansion and the tributary farms which are no longer in existence, Mount Vernon had to be self-sufficient.

An outstanding example is the spinning house on the north lane where 10 or more women were constantly employed spinning and knitting. Other buildings on the north lane are the greenhouse and quarters, icehouse, storehouse, gardener's house and museum.

Built in 1928, the museum houses a growing collection of Washington memorabilia and representative objects of the period. Included are a clay bust of Gen. Washington by the French sculptor, Jean Antoine Houdon, clothes worn by Gen. and Mrs. Washington and domestic items such as china.

Bowling Greens Divide Lanes

The north and south lanes are divided by the central bowling green with its luscious lawn, majestic trees and lovely shrubs. The south lane contains the butler's house, stable, smokehouse, washhouse and coachhouse. The latter three are open to the public.

Washington died December 14, 1799, in his bedroom on the second floor of the south addition to the mansion. He wrote these instructions in his will: "And it is my express desire that my corpse may be interred in a private manner, without ...parade or funeral oration." His wishes were respected and he is buried in a tomb in the vineyard enclosure.

Mount Vernon, overlooking the Potomac and low Maryland hills, is a beautiful sight. It is open to the public daily. But it would probably never have been restored if not for the efforts of Ann Pamela Cunningham and the Mount Vernon Ladies' Association.

COMMENTS ON THE ABOVE ARTICLE

* The paragraphs are short which is characteristic of newspaper style.
* The article is historical in tone. Mount Vernon is a historical place and the reader can get the feeling for the

times.
* The article conveys how George Washington loved Mount Vernon.
* The bold face subheadings break up the article.
* The article goes into some detail about the physical appearance of Mount Vernon. The reader can obtain a feeling of how lovely the place is.
* I think the article gives credit to women, in particular, the efforts of Ann Pamela Cunningham.
* With my byline (name), Journal Special Correspondent is mentioned. One might think that I wrote the article "on the spot". In reality, I wrote it after I returned from the trip.
* I like the main and secondary headings at the top of the article. It makes the reader want to read on.

And since I am on the subject of *The Milwaukee Journal* newspaper, here is their weekly magazine where a writer can sell a piece provided that he/she lives in Wisconsin. A description follows.

WISCONSIN, THE MILWAUKEE JOURNAL MAGAZINE

Wisconsin, The Milwaukee Journal Magazine - This weekly magazine, established in 1984, has a circulation of 530,000. It has from 16 to 88 pages.

Buys 80 to 100 manuscripts a year. Humor, profiles, personal experience and provocative essays are needed. Length from 750 to 2,500 words. Payment ranges from $75 to $500. Buys one-time rights.

How to break in: Read several issues to get a feel for *Wisconsin's* content. Then you might try a personal experience article, a thought-provoking or controversial essay or a lively profile. Also needed are 500 to 1,000 word fillers--social commentaries or slices of life that will touch readers. Most of *Wisconsin's* material comes from Wisconsin writers. It is not a good market for out-of-state writers but articles are bought from time to time from established writers outside of its circulation area.

Query the Editor at *Wisconsin, The Milwaukee Journal Magazine*, P. O. Box 661, Milwaukee, Wisconsin 53201-0661.

Here is an additional newspaper market with the types of freelance material wanted.

READER (R), CHICAGO'S FREE WEEKLY

Reader (R), Chicago's Free Weekly - Published weekly

except the last week of December. Roughly 70% of the editorial material in the *Reader* comes from freelance writers.

What kind of article is the *Reader* looking for? *The greatest need is for full-length magazine-style feature stories on Chicago topics.* Length should be at least 3,000 words, often more. Beyond saying this, the editor usually answers this question with a list of the things he is not looking for: hard news (What the Mayor Said About School Desegregation Yesterday); commentary and opinion (What I Think About What the Mayor Said About School Desegregation Yesterday); fiction; poetry; stories of national (as opposed to local) scope, or in celebrity for celebrity's sake (a la People, Rolling Stone). *Material is needed for these columns:* "Reading," "First Person," "Cityscope," "Sport," and "Neighborhood News" (material is needed once a month). Length of columns should be about 1,500 words. *Reviews of all types are needed.* They can be reviews on movies, pop music, theatre, dance, and opera. Length should be 1,200 words, preferably less. Writers should not be deceived by the fact that these reviews seem to be written by the same people every week. Reviews are sought from new writers who can do as well as or better than the regulars. *Material is needed for the calendar spread* (pages six and seven) which contains short articles of up to 700 words on places to go, things to do, restaurants, and shops. This is also a place for "Chi Lives" stories, short personality profiles on local people. This space is wide open to freelancers.

Payment ranges from $35 for record reviews to a maximum of $800 for the best features. Buys all rights unless an arrangement to the contrary is made before publication. Payment is sent before the 15th of the month following publication.

Send completed manuscripts to the Editor at the *Reader*, 11 E. Illinois, Chicago, Illinois 60611.

ABOUT THE AUTHOR

Ruth Wucherer has taught writing and travel writing classes at the YMCA, University of Wisconsin-Milwaukee and Marquette University's Division of Continuing Education. She currently is working on her Master's Degree in journalism at Marquette University and intends to graduate in August 1988.

This is her second book to be published by R&E Publishers. Her first book, titled *Travel Writing for Fun and Profit: How To Add Dollars To Your Income Writing Travel Articles and Getting Them Published*, was published in 1984. It is still available from the publisher. The book recently underwent a second printing. Ms. Wucherer has also authored another book, three booklets and numerous articles on travel, business and feature subjects.

She works at the University of Wisconsin-Milwaukee. Recently she started her own business, *Ruth's Writing and Speaking Service*. Ms. Wucherer is available to write books, booklets, brochures, articles, news releases and do advertising copywriting. She also speaks about nonfiction writing, travel writing and related topics at clubs, conferences, seminars, workshops and classes. Her fees are reasonable. If you are interested in having someone do writing or speaking before your group, contact Ms. Wucherer at 3045 S. 9th Place, Milwaukee, Wisconsin 53215.

Ms. Wucherer is a member of The Wisconsin Authors and Publishers Alliance, the Wisconsin Regional Writers Association and The International Women's Writing Guild.